2nd EDITION

Pupil Book 6A

T0312328

Series Editor: Peter Clarke

Authors: Elizabeth Jurgensen, Jeanette Mumford, Sandra Roberts, Linda Glithro

Contents

7-digit numbers

Read and write numbers to 10,000,000 and determine the value of each digit

 Challenge 1

1 Decompose each of these numbers to show the place value of each digit.

> **Example**
> 185,386 = 100,000 + 80,000 + 5,000 + 300 + 80 + 6

a	367,912	b	205,936	c	617,483
d	558,165	e	926,815	f	783,402
g	833,639	h	970,275	i	862,206

2 Choose four of the numbers from Question 1 and write them out in words.

 Challenge 2

1 Decompose each of these numbers to show the place value of each digit.

> **Example**
> 3,753,193 = 3,000,000 + 700,000 + 50,000 + 3,000 + 100 + 90 + 3

a	4,872,128	b	1,631,197	c	5,502,472	d	2,378,207
e	7,927,802	f	5,047,155	g	7,825,831	h	9,777,222

2 Choose four of the numbers from Question 1 and write them out in words.

3 Each of these cards represents the place value of a digit in a number. Compose ten 7-digit numbers using these cards.

| 5,000,000 | 700,000 | 200,000 | 80,000 |

| 10,000 | 6,000 | 4,000 |

| 300 | 50 | 90 | 6 |

| 3,000,000 | 800 | 1 |

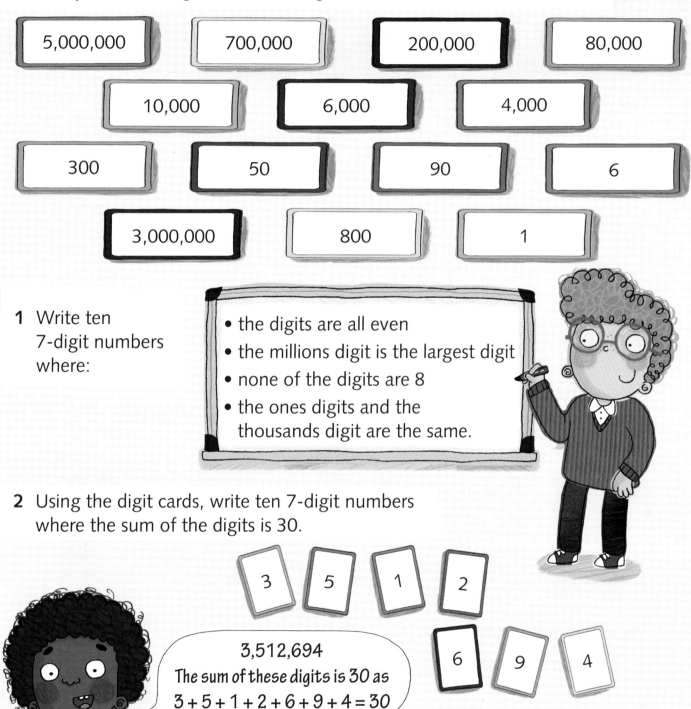

1 Write ten 7-digit numbers where:

- the digits are all even
- the millions digit is the largest digit
- none of the digits are 8
- the ones digits and the thousands digit are the same.

2 Using the digit cards, write ten 7-digit numbers where the sum of the digits is 30.

3   5   1   2

6   9   4

3,512,694
The sum of these digits is 30 as
3 + 5 + 1 + 2 + 6 + 9 + 4 = 30

3 Using the numbers you made in Question 2, play this game with a partner.

You will need:
- 0–9 dice

- Take turns to say a place value, for example, millions.
- Roll the dice. If you have that digit in the chosen place value, cross it out.
- The first player to cross out one whole number is the winner.

7-digit ordering

Compare and order numbers to 10,000,000 and determine
the value of each digit

Challenge
1

1 Order each set of numbers, smallest to largest.

a 487,397, 419,386, 463,297, 402,392, 453,927

b 783,297, 719,235, 773,227, 785,297, 760,383

c 279,385, 234,297, 285,268, 271,297, 237,251

d 659,286, 651,375, 658,295, 650,286, 658,296

e 305,286, 305,816, 305,047, 305,575, 305,773

f 596,287, 591,486, 562,286, 594,386, 561,386

g 837,393, 839,486, 837,083, 839,382, 837,187

h 993,365, 996,262, 993,261, 996,100, 993,325

i 324,751, 340,794, 315,888, 348,546, 312,135

j 96,104, 161,171, 107,356, 150,281, 137,790

> **Remember**
> When comparing and ordering numbers, start with the digits with the greatest place value – the most significant digits.

2 Write the next number.

a 562,349

b 403,499

c 608,369

d 199,999

e 725,439

f 640,589

g 714,329

h 268,009

i 692,449

j 511,479

1 Each set of numbers is in order. What could the missing numbers be?

a 2,398,363, 2,408,826, 2,489,275,   ,   , 2,496,887

b 5,400,250, 5,400,650, 5,400,850,   ,   , 5,400,999

c 7,654,000, 7,655,000, 7,656,000,   ,   , 7,676,000

d 3,154,782, 3,583,773, 3,591,375,   ,   , 3,592,406

e 6,247,222, 6,248,022, 6,248,200,   ,   , 6,249,582

f 9,736,187, 9,745,376, 9,750,075,   ,   , 9,755,010

g 4,000,000, 5,000,000, 6,000,000,   ,   , 9,000,000

h 8,408,383, 8,523,374, 8,583,750,   ,   , 8,583,820

i 7,401,916, 7,651,898, 7,822,620,   ,   , 7,822,630

j 1,878,096, 1,878,596, 1,878,637,   ,   , 1,878,642

2 Write the next number.

a 5,478,300   b 1,208,269   c 4,832,297

d 8,289,599   e 4,295,000   f 3,199,999

g 8,497,209   h 2,638,890   i 3,432,729

j 5,299,305   k 7,684,319   l 9,999,999

1 Use the digit cards to make ten different 7-digit numbers.

Hint
Organising your numbers in a systematic way will help you to check that you do not repeat any numbers.

2 Order your numbers, smallest to largest.

3 Explain how to order 7-digit numbers.

Rounding 7-digit numbers

Round any whole number to a required degree of accuracy

Example

(147,360)← 147,362 → 147,370

147,300 ← 147,362 → (147,400)

(147,000)← 147,362 → 148,000

Challenge 1

1 Write the multiples of 10, 100 and 1,000 that each number lies between.

a 265,892

b 487,371

c 306,385

d 725,247

e 846,794

f 532,766

g 921,653

h 798,518

i 642,386

2 For each of your answers in Question 1, circle the multiple that the number rounds to.

Challenge 2

1 Write the multiples of 10, 100 and 1,000 that each number lies between.

a 3,973,729

b 4,538,255

c 7,315,837

d 5,724,619

e 6,838,711

f 8,526,584

g 4,652,176

h 6,237,453

2 For each of your answers in Question 1, circle the multiple that the number rounds to.

3 For each of the numbers below, write three numbers that, when rounded down, equal the number. In brackets beside your numbers show the degree of rounding.

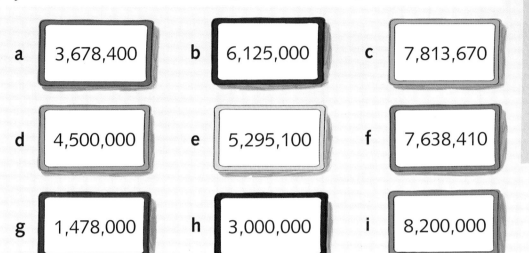

Example

5,684,700

5,684,701 (10)
5,684,728 (100)
5,684,685 (100)

a 3,678,400   **b** 6,125,000   **c** 7,813,670

d 4,500,000   **e** 5,295,100   **f** 7,638,410

g 1,478,000   **h** 3,000,000   **i** 8,200,000

nge

1 Write the multiples of 10,000, 100,000 and 1,000,000 that each number lies between.

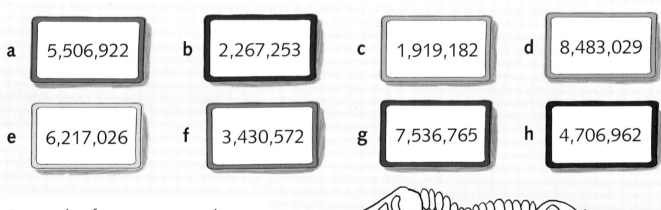

a 5,506,922   **b** 2,267,253   **c** 1,919,182   **d** 8,483,029

e 6,217,026   **f** 3,430,572   **g** 7,536,765   **h** 4,706,962

2 For each of your answers in Question 1, circle the multiple that the number rounds to.

3 In one year, a museum had 4,691,692 visitors and 1,456 complaints.

Write a report on behalf of the museum explaining these figures. Make sure that your report is worded in a way that looks best for the museum. You may want to round these numbers to different degrees.

When you've finished, write a statement explaining why you included these numbers in your report.

T-Rex

Changing digits

Solve number problems

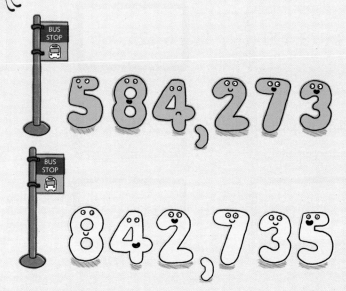

Challenge 1

This 6-digit number is standing at the bus stop:

If the first digit goes to the back of the queue, the new number will be:

a Copy the two numbers above. Imagine that the digits keep going to the back of the queue, one by one. Write the other four new numbers they will make.

b Look at your answers to Question **a**. The digit 5 had each of the values below. What is the total of these six values?

 500,000    5   50   500   5,000   50,000

c Write all the values and totals for these digits in your answers to Question **a**.

    i 8   **ii** 2   **iii** 7

d Explain the reason the totals are made up of the same digit.

Challenge 2

This 7-digit number is standing at the bus stop:

If the first digit goes to the back of the queue, the new number will be:

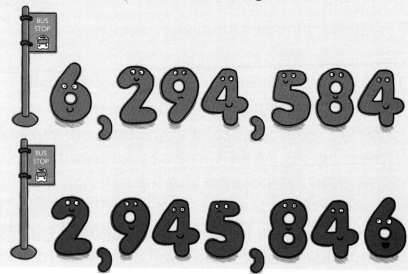

a Copy the two numbers. Imagine that the digits keep going to the back of the queue, one by one. Write the other five new numbers they will make.

b Look at your answers to Question **a**. The digit 6 had different values.
  i Write all the different values.
  ii What is the total of all the values?

c Write all the values and totals for these digits in your answers to Question **a**.
  i 9 **ii** 5 **iii** 8

d Explain the reason the totals are made up of the same digit.

e Explain why the values can all be added together mentally.

f Each time the first number moves to the back of the queue, each of the other digits increases in value.
  i By how much does the 5 increase each time?
  ii By how much does the 8 increase each time?
  iii What do you notice about your answers in **i** and **ii**? Explain why.

This 6-digit number is standing at the bus stop:

ge

You will need:
• calculator

791,864

If the first digit goes to the back of the queue, the new number will be:

918,647

a Add together the two numbers above.

b Is the answer a multiple of 11? Use a calculator to find out.

c Choose a different 6-digit number. Move the first digit to the back of the queue and add the two numbers together. Is the answer a multiple of 11? Can you prove this always happens?

Adding mentally

- Add mentally, including with large numbers
- Use estimation to check answers

Challenge I

Work out these calculations mentally. Show any working out.

a **376,154**
i + 7,000
ii + 850
iii + 42,000

b **603,147**
i + 580
ii + 31,000
iii + 6,000

c **568,743**
i + 6,000
ii + 17,000
iii + 630

d **750,862**
i + 7,100
ii + 46,000
iii + 460

e **862,774**
i + 910
ii + 5,600
iii + 51,000

f **937,927**
i + 9,000
ii + 67,000
iii + 580

Challenge 2

1 First estimate the answers to these calculations, then work them out mentally. Show any working out. Check your answer is close to your estimate.

a **2,387,590**
i + 60,000
ii + 300,000
iii + 540

b **1,206,472**
i + 43,000
ii + 5,100
iii + 500,000

c **4,517,640**
i + 950
ii + 600,000
iii + 4,000

d **3,865,413**
i + 400,000
ii + 7,200
iii + 830

e **6,731,604**
i + 840
ii + 700,000
iii + 3,800

f **5,145,355**
i + 5,500
ii + 400,000
iii + 700

2 What has been added each time to reach the next number?

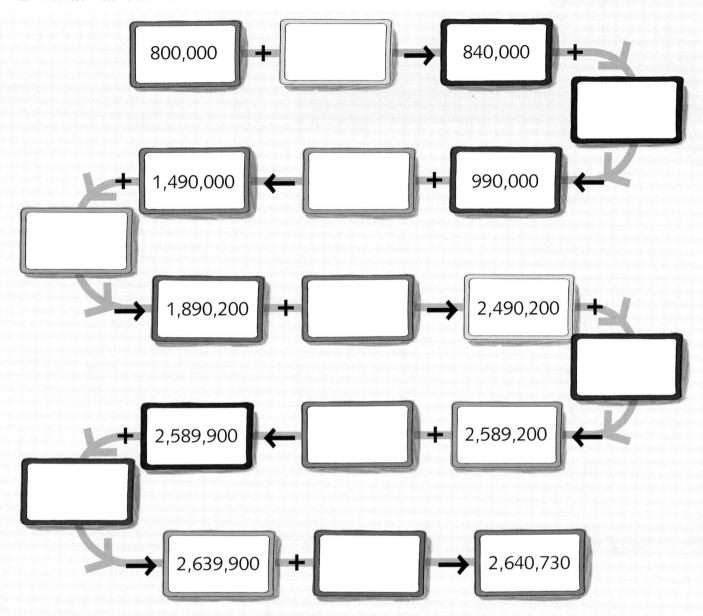

Work out the missing numbers mentally.

a 2,674,836 + ⬚ = 3,174,836   **b** 4,315,738 + ⬚ = 4,915,738

c 3,721,274 + ⬚ = 4,521,274   **d** 5,873,297 + ⬚ = 6,173,297

e 6,947,361 + ⬚ = 7,547,361   **f** 600,000 + ⬚ = 4,386,543

g 400,000 + ⬚ = 5,812,440   **h** 700,000 + ⬚ = 6,381,502

i 800,000 + ⬚ = 3,491,532   **j** 900,000 + ⬚ = 1,582,365

Subtracting mentally

- Subtract mentally, including with large numbers
- Use estimation to check answers

Challenge 1

Work out these calculations mentally. Show any working out.

a | 248,386

i – 4,000
ii – 230
iii – 31,000

b | 563,845

i – 730
ii – 45,000
iii – 5,000

c | 681,378

i – 7,000
ii – 27,000
iii – 640

d | 463,822

i – 3,100
ii – 35,000
iii – 750

e | 754,233

i – 580
ii – 6,200
iii – 41,000

f | 855,912

i – 560
ii – 38,000
iii – 7,100

Challenge 2

1 First estimate the answers to these calculations, then work them out mentally. Show your working out. Check your answer is close to your estimate.

a | 3,763,282

i – 50,000
ii – 200,000
iii – 240

b | 4,738,295

i – 29,000
ii – 4,800
iii – 400,000

c | 6,287,674

i – 710
ii – 400,000
iii – 8,000

d | 7,590,217

i – 600,000
ii – 1,200
iii – 210

e | 5,493,751

i – 760
ii – 700,000
iii – 4,800

f | 8,691,302

i – 25,000
ii – 1,200
iii – 250

2 What has been subtracted each time to reach the next number?

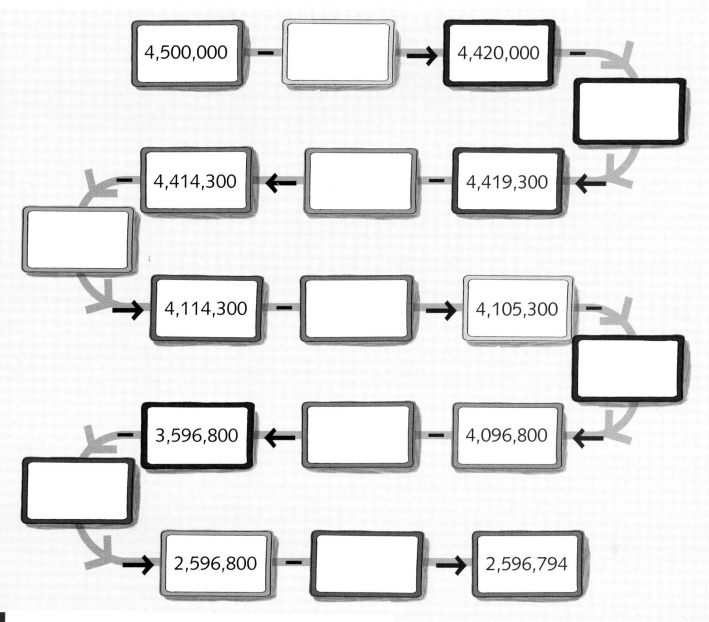

4,500,000 − ☐ → 4,420,000 − ☐ →

☐ ← 4,419,300 − ☐ ← 4,414,300 ← ☐ −

☐ → 4,114,300 − ☐ → 4,105,300 − ☐

4,096,800 − ☐ ← 3,596,800 − ☐

☐ → 2,596,800 − ☐ → 2,596,794

1 Work out the missing numbers mentally.

a 3,428,827 − ☐ = 2,928,827   **b** 4,398,291 − ☐ = 3,898,291

c 2,864,375 − ☐ = 2,828,375   **d** 6,721,453 − ☐ = 6,121,453

e 8,836,525 − ☐ = 7,836,525   **f** 7,329,081 − ☐ = 6,729,081

2 Explain how you worked out the missing numbers in Question 1.

3 When do you think mental calculations should be used and when should written calculations be used? In your opinion, is it important to know how to calculate mentally and use a written method? Explain why.

Adding and subtracting decimals (1)

Add and subtract decimals mentally

Challenge 1

Add and subtract these decimals mentally.

a	37·4 + 25·8	**b**	19·7 + 42·6	**c**	39·8 + 45·4
d	68·9 + 32·7	**e**	61·4 + 56·8	**f**	72·3 + 45·9
g	38·6 + 73·5	**h**	59·4 + 57·9	**i**	65·3 + 78·4
j	62·4 – 38·2	**k**	71·6 – 53·4	**l**	85·6 – 31·8
m	74·1 – 46·5	**n**	87·5 – 27·8	**o**	90·2 – 53·4
p	72·7 – 48·8	**q**	95·3 – 68·6	**r**	52·4 – 28·6

Challenge 2

1 Add and subtract these decimals mentally.

a	63·48 + 29·29	**b**	39·63 + 52·48
c	58·26 + 57·5	**d**	97·8 + 32·19
e	61·48 + 79·59	**f**	87·4 + 95·98
g	89·08 + 76·97	**h**	65·4 + 92·63
i	58·32 – 31·53	**j**	62·47 – 45·82
k	71·61 – 55·4	**l**	86·4 – 27·51
m	94·13 – 45·35	**n**	82·38 – 37·5
o	72·2 – 33·86	**p**	99·04 – 48·37

Remember

We can apply place value knowledge to known addition and subtraction facts to add and subtract tenths and hundredths.

Remember to use jottings to help you.

2 Each set of three circles total the number in the square. Work out the missing numbers.

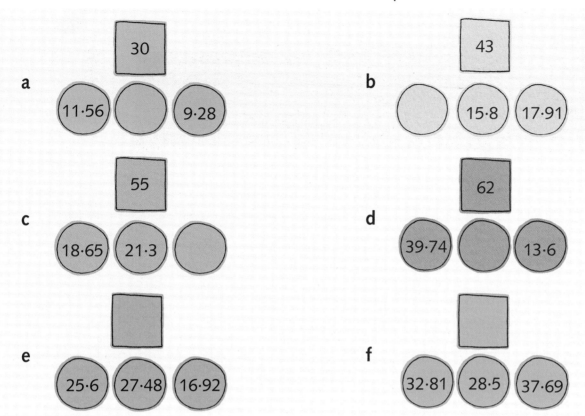

a

30

11·56   ( )   9·28

b

43

( )   15·8   17·91

c

55

18·65   21·3   ( )

d

62

39·74   ( )   13·6

e

( )

25·6   27·48   16·92

f

( )

32·81   28·5   37·69

The three decimal numbers along each side total the number in the circle.
Work out the missing numbers.

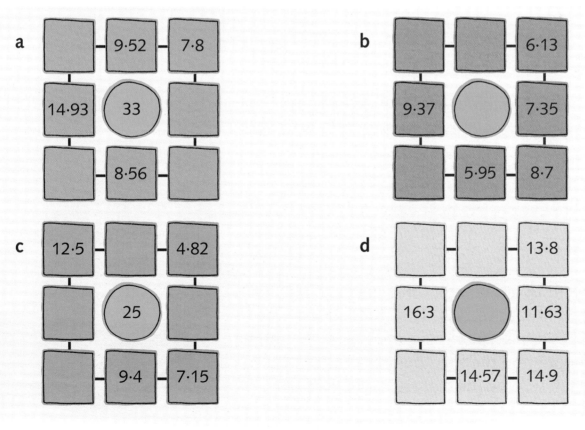

a

9·52 — 7·8

14·93   33

8·56

b

6·13

9·37   ( )   7·35

5·95 — 8·7

c

12·5 — — 4·82

25

9·4 — 7·15

d

13·8

16·3   ( )   11·63

14·57 — 14·9

Museum problems

- Solve multi-step problems in contexts, deciding which operations and methods to use and why
- Use estimation to check accuracy of answers

Challenge 1

Answer these museum problems.

a A science museum had 653,760 visitors last year. If there were 230,000 child visitors and 147,000 senior citizens visitors and the rest were adults, how many adult visitors were there?

b In a survey, 4,578 people took part. One third of them said they thought it was the best museum they had visited. How many people thought this?

c During one week in winter, 5,845 visitors wore pairs of gloves. How many gloves were there at the museum that week?

d One day the museum guide was on special offer for £3. The shop sold 936 copies. How much money was taken from the sale of these?

e On the busiest day of the year there were 7,406 visitors. On the quietest day there were 1,620 visitors. What was the difference between the visitor numbers on these two days?

Challenge 2

1 Answer these museum problems.

a A natural history museum had 2,653,812 visitors last year. A quarter of them were senior citizens, 900,000 were children and the rest were adults. How many adults visited the museum?

b In the gift shop, a profit of £5,673.78 was made in one week. The next week was very busy and double that amount of profit was made. What was the total profit made in those two weeks?

c The museum bought three new exhibits for the dinosaur section. Their total spend was £856,400. Two of the exhibits cost the same amount and the third one cost £270,000. What was the price of each of the other two exhibits?

d The museum's budget for new signs is £6,500. Each sign costs £6. The museum buys as many signs as it can. How much money is left?

e The manager spent £768,429 on decorating the museum. He spent £325,350 on the education centre and the rest on three of the exhibition rooms. How much was spent on each exhibition room?

2 Write your own museum problems based on these calculations.

a 1,678,390 – 40,000 – 780

b 395,270 + 900,000 + 30,000

c £7,629.25 + £2,958.10 – £3,861.02

Answer these museum problems.

a The museum manager is working out the visitor numbers for last year. When he adds the children, senior citizens and adult visitor numbers together it totals 3,652,780. When he adds the children and senior citizens together it totals 1,976,000. When he adds the children and adults together it totals 2,376,788. How many of each kind of visitor were there?

b Heating and cooling the museum costs £23,475 for the three coldest months, £18,781 for the three hottest months and £31,547 for the other six months.

   i What is the total annual bill?

   ii What is the average heating bill for one of the coldest months?

   iii The museum gets a 10% discount on its annual energy bill. What is the new cost?

c The museum exceeds its gift shop sales target by 25%. £450,000 was the total profit. What was the museum's target?

d After a trip to the museum, teachers at a school want to buy some books to support their topics. They spend a total of £165.20. £78.50 was spent on dinosaur books and £35.99 on a very special Atlas. With the rest of the money, they bought as many insect books costing £12.30 as they could. How much money was left?

Building 3-D shapes

Build 3-D shapes from 2-D drawings

You will need:
- interlocking cubes in two colours

1 Look at the shapes below and write how many of each 2-D face the 3-D shapes have.

2-D faces

3-D shapes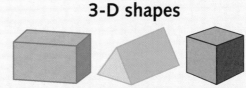

a cuboid   **b** triangular prism   **c** cube

2 Build each shape below, in turn, with interlocking cubes of the same colour. Follow the instructions for each shape.

- Work out the least number of additional cubes you will need to make the shape into a cuboid.
- Using a different colour, add that number of cubes to the shape to check that you are correct. Write how many cubes you needed.

A 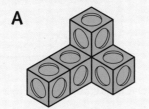   B 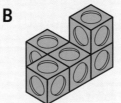   C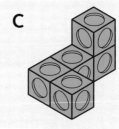

1 Build each shape below, in turn, with interlocking cubes of the same colour. Follow the instructions for each shape.

- Work out the least number of additional cubes you will need to make the shape into a cuboid.
- Using a different colour, add that number of cubes to the shape to check that you are correct. Write how many cubes you needed.

A 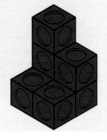   B    C

2 Build each shape below, in turn, with interlocking cubes of the same colour. Follow the instructions for each shape.

- For each shape, predict the least number of additional cubes you will need to build all the layers of the shape up to one level higher than the highest end.
- Using a different colour, add that number of cubes to the shape to check that you are correct. Write how many cubes you needed.

A 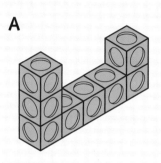 **B** 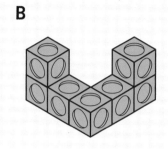 **C**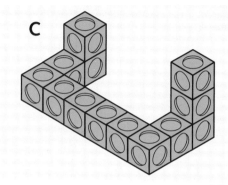

enge

1 Work with a partner. Build each tower, in turn, with interlocking cubes of the same colour. Follow the instructions for each shape.

- Work out the least number of additional cubes you will need to make each tower into a cube.
- Using a different colour, add that number of cubes to the tower to check that you are correct.

A 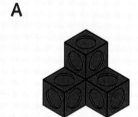 **B** 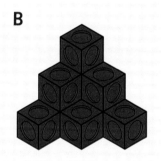 **C**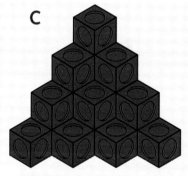

2 Use your work from Question 1 to answer the questions.

a Copy and complete the table.

Shape	Number of cubes in tower	Number of cubes added	Total number of cubes
A			8 or 2 × 2 × 2
B			
C			

b Look for a pattern. Work out the total number of cubes needed to build cube D.

21

Nets of open and closed cubes

Identify and build different nets for an open or a closed cube

Challenge 1

The pictures below show five different designs on each face of an open cube.

You will need:
- 1 cm squared paper
- ruler
- scissors

Here are four views of the open cube:

- Copy the net on the right onto 1 cm squared paper. Make the side of each face 5 cm long.
- Draw the faces in the correct place to make the open cube.
- Cut out and fold up the net to check your answer.

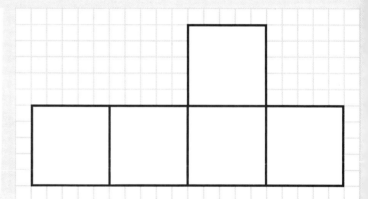

Challenge 2

Some of the shapes on the opposite page are nets of closed cubes.

- Copy the table below.
- Make each shape, in turn, with your interlocking squares. Then fold the shape up to see if it makes a cube.
- For each shape, enter ✓ if the shape is a net of a cube and ✗ if it is not.

You will need:
- six interlocking squares

Shape	A	B	C	D	E	F	G	H	I	J	K	L
Net of a cube												

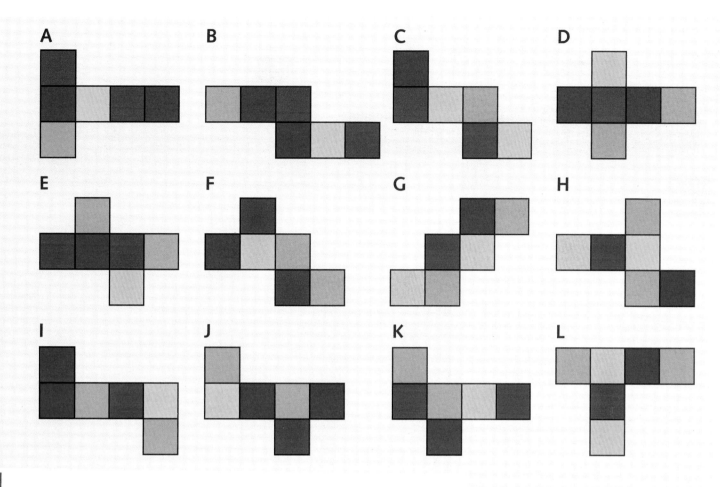

Make two copies of each of the nets below onto 1 cm square paper. Make the side of each face 5 cm long. Each one is the net of an open cube. The shaded square is the bottom face.

- For each net find two different ways to add one square and turn it into the net of a closed cube.

- Cut out each net, with the square added, and check that it will fold into a cube.

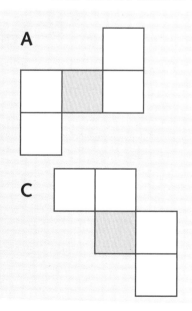

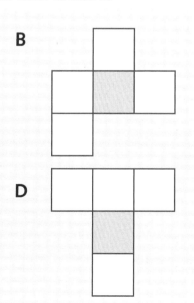

23

Nets of a cube and a cuboid

Construct nets for a cube and a cuboid

You will need:
- 1 cm square dot grid paper
- ruler
- scissors
- glue

Challenge 1

Build a cube.

- Copy the net of the cube onto 1 cm square dot grid paper. Draw the seven tabs as shown.
- Carefully cut out the net.
- Score along each fold line using a ruler and scissors.
- Fold along each fold line and assemble the shape by gluing each tab in turn. The last face to stick down is the one without any tabs.

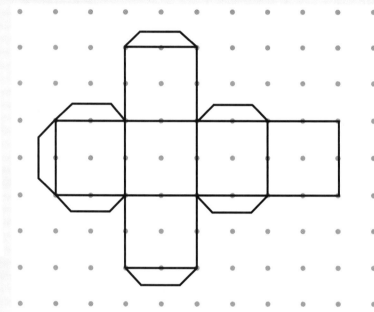

Challenge 2

1 Build a dice.

- Copy the net of the dice onto 1 cm square dot grid paper. Draw the seven tabs as shown and copy the dots.
- Fill in the missing dots so that opposite faces add to 7.
- Cut out the net, score and fold along the fold lines and assemble the shape by gluing the tabs in turn. The last face to stick down is the one without any tabs.

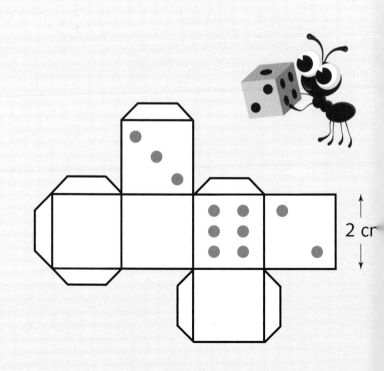

2 cm

2 Build a cuboid.

- Using the lengths of sides as shown in the diagram, copy the net of the cuboid onto 1 cm square dot grid paper.
- Decide where to draw the seven tabs.
- Cut out the net, score and fold along the fold lines and assemble the shape by gluing the tabs in turn. The last face to stick down is the one without any tabs.

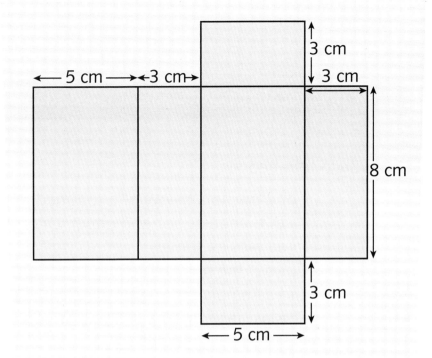

The edges of this cube measure 2 cm.
A spot covers one vertex of the cube.

For each of the nets below:

- copy the net onto 1 cm square dot grid paper
- add the two remaining parts of the spot so that the three parts will meet at the same vertex when the cube is made up
- decide where to draw the seven tabs
- cut out the nets and fold them up to check your spots match up.

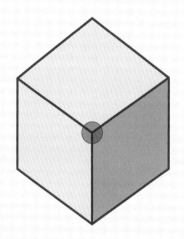

A

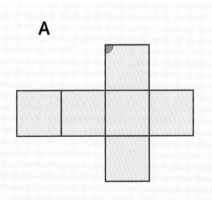

B

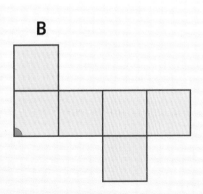

C

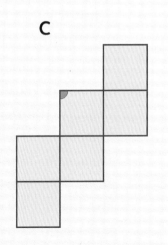

25

Nets for 3-D shapes with triangular faces

Draw nets for shapes with one or more triangular faces

Challenge 1

Build tetrahedons.

- Copy the nets below of a tetrahedron onto 1 cm triangular dot grid paper. Draw each set of three tabs as shown.
- Cut out the nets, score and fold along the fold lines and assemble the shapes by gluing the tabs in turn. The last face to stick down is the one without any tabs.

You will need:
- 1 cm triangular dot grid paper
- ruler
- scissors
- glue

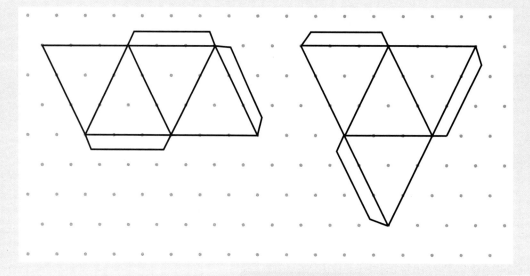

Challenge 2

1 Build an octahedron.

- Copy the net of the octahedron onto 1 cm triangular dot grid paper. Draw the five tabs as shown.
- Cut out the net, score and fold along the fold lines and assemble the shape by gluing the tabs in turn. The last face to stick down is the one without any tabs.

You will need:
- 1 cm triangular dot grid paper • ruler
- scissors • glue • coloured pencils

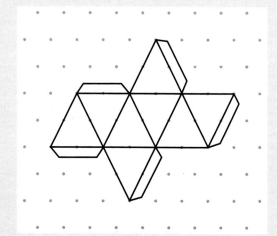

2 Work with a partner. Each person should copy and cut out the net below of a square-based pyramid. Find a way to stick both of your shapes together to make a 'snap dragon' octahedron. Add the teeth and the eyes.

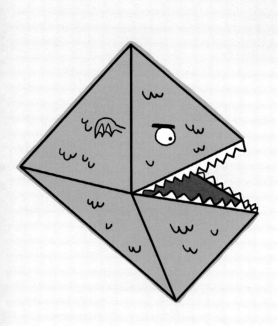

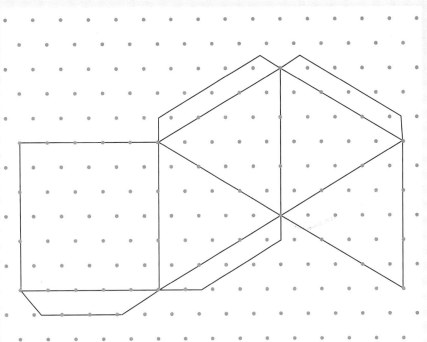

1 Work with a partner. Each person should construct a square-based pyramid using the net shown.

- Draw a square with sides of 6 cm.
- Using your ruler and protractor, draw an equilateral triangle with sides of 6 cm on each side of the square.
- Draw a tab on one side of each triangle.
- Cut out the net, score and fold along the fold lines and glue the tabs in turn to form the square-based pyramid.

You will need:
- sheet of paper
- protractor
- ruler
- scissors
- glue

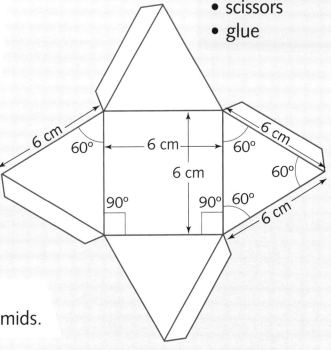

2 Name the 3-D shape you can make using both of your square-based pyramids.

Multiplying ThHTO × O

- Use the formal written method of short multiplication to calculate ThHTO × O
- Estimate and check the answer to a calculation

Example

50 × 9 = 450

Challenge 1

Write the multiplication fact for each number in the sets below.

× 9

90	50
300	80
700	6
40	1,200
20	110

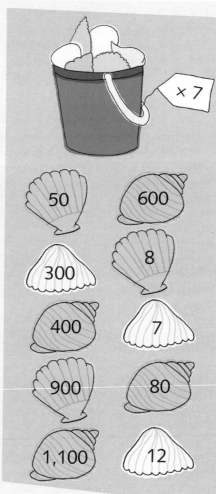

× 7

50	600
300	8
400	7
900	80
1,100	12

× 6

	90
700	
80	12
6	50
400	600
120	110

Challenge 2

1 Work out the answer to these calculations. Show any working out.

a 26 × 3 × 7 × 4   b 64 × 6 × 8   c 53 × 5 × 4

d 32 × 6 × 8 × 4   e 27 × 5 × 9 × 6   f 47 × 9 × 8 × 3

g 68 × 4 × 9 × 9   h 25 × 5 × 5 × 5   i 17 × 6 × 4 × 9

2 Play this game with a partner.

Take turns to:

- Choose a number from the number cards below and write it down (you can only use each number once).
- Roll the dice.
- Multiply your chosen number by the number rolled on the dice, estimating your answer first.
- Calculate the answer using the formal written method.
- Check that your answer is close to your estimate.

The player with the larger answer scores one point.
The first player to score five points is the winner.

You will need:
- 0–9 dice

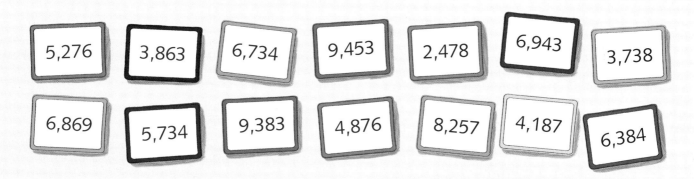

5,276   3,863   6,734   9,453   2,478   6,943   3,738

6,869   5,734   9,383   4,876   8,257   4,187   6,384

Work out the unknown numbers in these calculations.

a
```
    □ 3 □ 8
  ×       □
  _____
  2 1 □ 4 0
```

b
```
  6 □ 6 □
  ×     7
  _____
  4 □ 3 □ 9
```

c
```
    □ 5 0 □
  ×       □
  _____
  6 7 5 5 4
```

d
```
  □ □ 0 □
  ×     4
  _____
  3 □ 8 □ 4
```

e
```
  4 □ □ 8
  ×     6
  _____
  2 □ 2 2 □
```

f
```
  8 □ 6 □
  ×     7
  _____
  5 □ 2 □ 7
```

Multiplication TO × TO using the expanded written method

- Use the expanded written method of long multiplication to calculate TO × TO
- Estimate and check the answer to a calculation

Challenge 1

Work out these multiplication calculations.

1 a 8 × 3
   b 80 × 30
   c 8 × 30

2 a 9 × 8
   b 80 × 9
   c 90 × 80

3 a 7 × 4
   b 70 × 4
   c 40 × 70

4 a 8 × 6
   b 6 × 80
   c 80 × 60

5 a 8 × 8
   b 80 × 80
   c 80 × 8

6 a 9 × 30
   b 3 × 9
   c 30 × 90

7 a 6 × 5
   b 60 × 5
   c 60 × 50

8 a 7 × 8
   b 70 × 80
   c 80 × 70

Challenge 2

1 Choose a number from each box below and create a multiplication calculation. Estimate the answer first. Multiply the numbers together using the expanded written method. Then compare your answer with your estimate. Choose different numbers each time. Write at least eight calculations.

Example

$43 \times 38 \rightarrow 40 \times 40 = 1{,}600$

```
        4 3
   ×    3 8
        2 4    (3 × 8)
      3 2 0    (40 × 8)
        9 0    (3 × 30)
    1 2 0 0    (40 × 30)
    1 6 3 4
        1
```

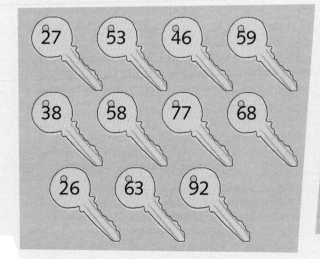

2 Make your own TO × TO calculations. Choose any two numbers from below. Multiply them together. Choose another two numbers. Multiply them together. Multiply the answers from both of your calculations to get your final answer. Try this five times.

Use each of the digit cards once. Make a calculation that gives the answer shown.

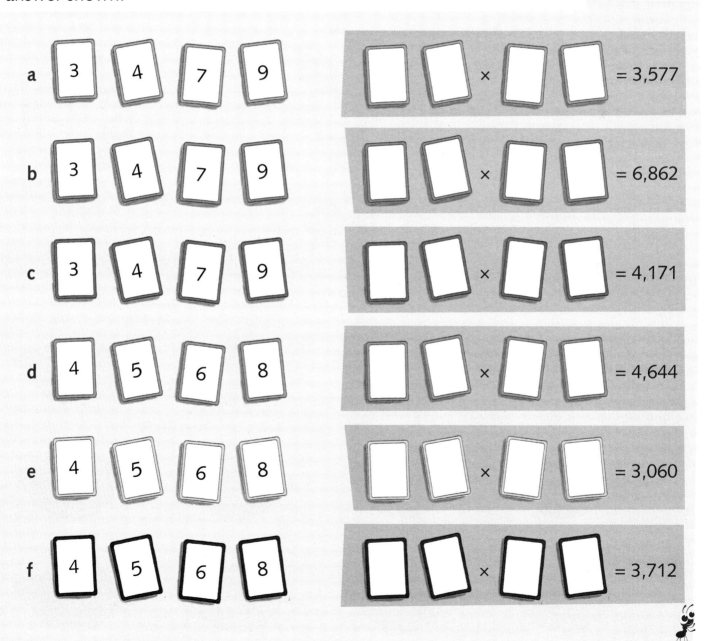

a 3 4 7 9 ☐☐ × ☐☐ = 3,577

b 3 4 7 9 ☐☐ × ☐☐ = 6,862

c 3 4 7 9 ☐☐ × ☐☐ = 4,171

d 4 5 6 8 ☐☐ × ☐☐ = 4,644

e 4 5 6 8 ☐☐ × ☐☐ = 3,060

f 4 5 6 8 ☐☐ × ☐☐ = 3,712

Multiplication TO × TO using the formal written method

- Use the formal written method of long multiplication to calculate TO × TO
- Estimate and check the answer to a calculation

Challenge 1

1 Work out the missing number in each multiplication fact.

a   7 × 9 =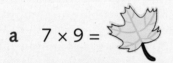

b   × 7 = 49

c   8 × 6 =

d   9 × = 108

e   4 × = 48

f   7 × = 42

g   6 × = 54

h   × 8 = 72

i   × 8 = 32

j   9 × = 63

k   7 × = 28

l   6 × = 36

2 Work out the answer to each calculation mentally.

a   60 × 7

b   50 × 80

c   60 × 8

d   9 × 70

e   80 × 9

f   80 × 7

g   3 × 80

h   90 × 50

i   60 × 90

j   40 × 40

k   70 × 60

l   30 × 40

Estimate the answer first, then use the formal written method to calculate the answer to each calculation.

a 45 × 42

b 68 × 68

c 76 × 67

d 38 × 49

e 57 × 39

f 61 × 83

g 72 × 51

h 87 × 58

i 76 × 77

j 26 × 64

k 37 × 78

l 84 × 48

m 55 × 55

n 65 × 56

o 18 × 81

1 Work out the missing digits in each calculation.

a ☐7 × 3☐ = 891

b 2☐ × 84 = ☐,184

c 36 × 6☐ = 2,☐48

d 38 × ☐9 = 1,862

e ☐6 × 56 = 3,136

f 4☐ × 47 = 2,021

g 29 × ☐1 = 2,059

h 35 × ☐☐ = 8☐5

2 Write two different TO × TO calculations that give each of these answers.

1,944   896   1,012   720   988

Solving word problems (1)

Solve problems involving addition, subtraction, multiplication and division

Challenge 1

Copy each calculation and write the missing sign.

a 60 ___ 80 = 4,800

b 600 = 12 ___ 50

c 10 = 90 ___ 80

d 1,500 ___ 300 = 1,200

e 640 ___ 80 = 8

f 70 ___ 80 = 5,600

g 3 ___ 80 = 240

h 760 ___ 120 = 880

i 310 ___ 30 = 280

j 120 ___ 30 = 4

k 480 ___ 8 = 60

l 500 ___ 50 = 10

Challenge 2

A school has to purchase some new items. Work out the answer to each question.

£49

kettle

£38

globe

£36

set of 6 novels

£28

box of paints

£56

telephone

£39

tennis racquet

a The school buys 48 novels altogether. How much does it spend?

b A school buys 24 globes. How much change does the school receive from £1,000?

c The supplier has a sale: 'Buy one get one half price'. The school office buys 6 kettles. How much is spent?

d It is decided that each classroom needs a new telephone. There are 24 classrooms. What is the total cost?

e Tennis racquets are on sale at one third off their original price. If the school buys 36, how much does it spend?

f One of each item is purchased. What is the total cost?

g Novels are sold separately for £7 each. The library buys 3,465 separate novels over the year. What is the total cost?

h Your class has a budget of £500 to spend. What would you buy?

1 Using the information in Challenge 2, work out the answers to these problems.

a Janet buys two of the same item. She pays with two £50 notes and gets £24 change. What item does she buy?

b The two Year 6 classes spend the same amount of money on items. One class buys 3 boxes of paints. The other class buys 2 different items totalling the same amount of money. What items did they buy?

c All of the items shown are on sale at a 10% discount. What is the new price of each item? Record each calculation you make.

2 Investigate the following TO × TO puzzle.

- Look carefully at the digits in these two calculations. What do you notice?

48 × 42   24 × 84

- Work out the answer to both of the calculations. What do you notice?
- Work out the missing digits in this pair of calculations so the same thing happens.

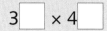

3☐ × 4☐   ☐4 × ☐3

- Can you make your own pairs of calculations that follow the same rule and have the same answer?

Fractions, factors and multiples (1)

- Use common factors to simplify fractions
- Use common multiples to express fractions in the same denominators

Challenge
1

1 Simplify these fractions.

Example

$$\frac{12}{15} = \frac{4}{5}$$

Both numbers have a factor of 3, so if I divide them both by 3, I get the simplified fraction $\frac{4}{5}$.

a $\frac{4}{10}$　　b $\frac{6}{15}$　　c $\frac{9}{12}$　　d $\frac{10}{20}$

e $\frac{8}{20}$　　f $\frac{10}{30}$　　g $\frac{12}{18}$　　h $\frac{8}{32}$

i $\frac{9}{27}$　　j $\frac{14}{16}$　　k $\frac{20}{30}$　　l $\frac{16}{28}$

m $\frac{12}{15}$　　n $\frac{18}{22}$　　o $\frac{16}{24}$　　p $\frac{15}{21}$

2 Write some fractions for a partner to simplify. Make sure you know the answers!

1 Play this game with a partner.

You will need:
• 1–6 dice

- Choose one of the fractions below and both write it down.
- Take turns to roll the dice.
- Simplify the fraction by the number you roll.
  If you cannot, wait for your next turn.
- Keep going until one player has the simplest form of the fraction. This scores one point.
- Play again, choosing other fractions from below. The first player to reach five points is the winner.

$\frac{40}{60}$ $\frac{48}{60}$ $\frac{24}{30}$ $\frac{30}{42}$ $\frac{24}{40}$

$\frac{36}{48}$ $\frac{56}{80}$ $\frac{18}{36}$ $\frac{50}{60}$ $\frac{48}{80}$

2 Choose two of the fractions below and change them to fractions with the same denominators. Do this ten times with different pairs of fractions. Fractions can be used more than once, but not in the same pair.

Example

$\frac{7}{10}$ and $\frac{4}{15}$

$\frac{7}{10} \overset{\times 3}{\underset{\times 3}{=}} \frac{21}{30}$ $\frac{4}{15} \overset{\times 2}{\underset{\times 2}{=}} \frac{8}{30}$

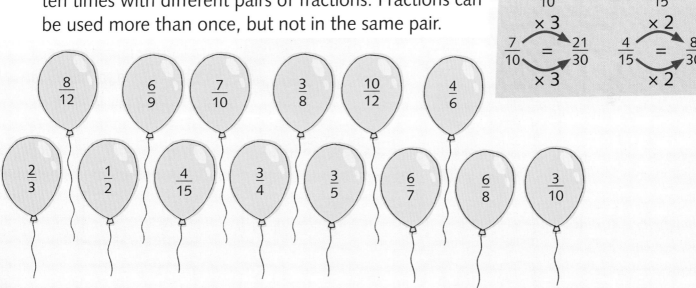

$\frac{8}{12}$ $\frac{6}{9}$ $\frac{7}{10}$ $\frac{3}{8}$ $\frac{10}{12}$ $\frac{4}{6}$

$\frac{2}{3}$ $\frac{1}{2}$ $\frac{4}{15}$ $\frac{3}{4}$ $\frac{3}{5}$ $\frac{6}{7}$ $\frac{6}{8}$ $\frac{3}{10}$

1 What is a simplified fraction?

2 Explain why $\frac{13}{15}$ cannot be simplified.

3 Roll a 0–9 dice four times and record your digits. If you roll zero, roll the dice again. Use the digits to make two proper fractions. Look at the denominators. Express the fractions as two fractions with the same denominator.

You will need:
• 0–9 dice

Ordering fractions

Compare and order fractions, including fractions greater than 1

Challenge 1

1 Order the fractions in each set, smallest to largest.

a $\frac{5}{6}$ $\frac{2}{3}$ $\frac{9}{12}$

b $\frac{1}{2}$ $\frac{5}{8}$ $\frac{3}{4}$

c $\frac{4}{6}$ $\frac{5}{9}$ $\frac{1}{3}$

d $\frac{1}{4}$ $\frac{3}{8}$ $\frac{2}{12}$

e $\frac{3}{5}$ $\frac{4}{10}$ $\frac{1}{2}$

f $\frac{3}{4}$ $\frac{7}{12}$ $\frac{2}{3}$

g $\frac{4}{7}$ $\frac{2}{3}$ $\frac{1}{2}$ h $\frac{4}{10}$ $\frac{1}{4}$ $\frac{2}{5}$

i $\frac{13}{16}$ $\frac{7}{8}$ $\frac{3}{4}$ j $\frac{2}{6}$ $\frac{3}{8}$ $\frac{1}{4}$

k $\frac{7}{10}$ $\frac{3}{5}$ $\frac{3}{4}$ l $\frac{4}{9}$ $\frac{1}{3}$ $\frac{1}{4}$

Example

$\frac{3}{4}$ → 4, 8, <u>12</u> $\frac{3}{4} = \frac{9}{12}$

$\frac{2}{3}$ → 3, 6, 9, <u>12</u> $\frac{2}{3} = \frac{8}{12}$

$\frac{1}{2}$ → 2, 4, 6, 8, 10, <u>12</u> $\frac{1}{2} = \frac{6}{12}$

$\frac{1}{2}, \frac{2}{3}, \frac{3}{4}$

> Remember to count on in steps of the denominator, to find the lowest common multiple. Then you can begin to put them in order.

2 Write a set of instructions explaining how to order fractions so you can remember how to do it.

1 For each set of fractions below, predict their order, smallest to largest, without converting them.

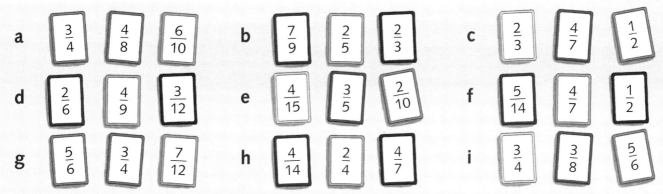

a $\frac{3}{4}$ $\frac{4}{8}$ $\frac{6}{10}$ b $\frac{7}{9}$ $\frac{2}{5}$ $\frac{2}{3}$ c $\frac{2}{3}$ $\frac{4}{7}$ $\frac{1}{2}$

d $\frac{2}{6}$ $\frac{4}{9}$ $\frac{3}{12}$ e $\frac{4}{15}$ $\frac{3}{5}$ $\frac{2}{10}$ f $\frac{5}{14}$ $\frac{4}{7}$ $\frac{1}{2}$

g $\frac{5}{6}$ $\frac{3}{4}$ $\frac{7}{12}$ h $\frac{4}{14}$ $\frac{2}{4}$ $\frac{4}{7}$ i $\frac{3}{4}$ $\frac{3}{8}$ $\frac{5}{6}$

2 Order each set of fractions in Question 1 by finding their lowest common denominator. Check to see if your predictions were close.

3 Order these improper fractions.

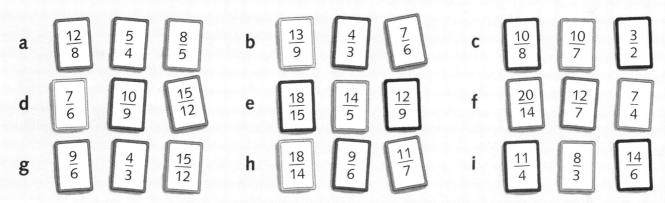

a $\frac{12}{8}$ $\frac{5}{4}$ $\frac{8}{5}$ b $\frac{13}{9}$ $\frac{4}{3}$ $\frac{7}{6}$ c $\frac{10}{8}$ $\frac{10}{7}$ $\frac{3}{2}$

d $\frac{7}{6}$ $\frac{10}{9}$ $\frac{15}{12}$ e $\frac{18}{15}$ $\frac{14}{5}$ $\frac{12}{9}$ f $\frac{20}{14}$ $\frac{12}{7}$ $\frac{7}{4}$

g $\frac{9}{6}$ $\frac{4}{3}$ $\frac{15}{12}$ h $\frac{18}{14}$ $\frac{9}{6}$ $\frac{11}{7}$ i $\frac{11}{4}$ $\frac{8}{3}$ $\frac{14}{6}$

Some proper fractions have been muddled up. Some of the numbers below are numerators and some are denominators of proper fractions that have been separated.

24 4 9 11 6 2 12 5 88 27 3 15

a Make a set of proper fractions using all the cards. Order your fractions, smallest to largest, by finding their common denominator.

b What were the smallest and largest fractions you could make?

c Look at your fractions again. Can you order them without converting them to common denominators?

d What strategy did you use to order your fractions in Question c? Compare your fractions and your strategy with a partner's. Did you make the same fractions?

Adding fractions

Add fractions with different denominators and mixed numbers, using the concept of equivalent fractions

Challenge 1

1 Add these mixed numbers. Show your working.

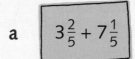

a $3\frac{2}{5} + 7\frac{1}{5}$

b $5\frac{1}{4} + 7\frac{2}{4}$

c $6\frac{5}{8} + 4\frac{2}{8}$

d $7\frac{3}{9} + 6\frac{5}{9}$

e $5\frac{4}{10} + 3\frac{5}{10}$

f $2\frac{2}{3} + 5\frac{1}{3}$

g $8\frac{2}{7} + 6\frac{4}{7}$

h $9\frac{1}{2} + 5\frac{1}{2}$

i $5\frac{3}{12} + 4\frac{5}{12}$

j $7\frac{5}{11} + 8\frac{5}{11}$

Example

$2\frac{3}{6} + 5\frac{2}{6}$

$2 + 5 = 7$

$\frac{3}{6} + \frac{2}{6} = \frac{5}{6}$

$7 + \frac{5}{6} = 7\frac{5}{6}$

> Add the whole numbers and then the fractions.

2 Add these fractions and then convert the answer to a mixed number.

a $\frac{3}{4} + \frac{3}{4}$

b $\frac{4}{5} + \frac{3}{5}$

c $\frac{5}{7} + \frac{4}{7}$

d $\frac{7}{8} + \frac{3}{8}$

e $\frac{7}{9} + \frac{7}{9}$

f $\frac{4}{7} + \frac{6}{7}$

g $\frac{8}{10} + \frac{6}{10}$

h $\frac{9}{11} + \frac{5}{11}$

i $\frac{7}{12} + \frac{6}{12}$

Example

$\frac{3}{6} + \frac{5}{6} = \frac{8}{6}$

$= 1\frac{2}{6}$

$= 1\frac{1}{3}$

Challenge 2

1 Add these mixed numbers.

a $3\frac{4}{5} + 6\frac{3}{5}$

b $2\frac{6}{8} + 4\frac{5}{8}$

c $6\frac{2}{3} + 8\frac{2}{3}$

d $5\frac{4}{9} + 7\frac{6}{9}$

e $6\frac{7}{10} + 8\frac{5}{10}$

f $9\frac{3}{4} + 5\frac{3}{4}$

g $3\frac{11}{13} + 6\frac{2}{13}$

h $8\frac{4}{7} + 5\frac{6}{7}$

i $9\frac{8}{12} + 7\frac{5}{12}$

j $3\frac{6}{13} + 7\frac{11}{13}$

2 Choose two of the mixed numbers below and add them together. Do this ten times. The mixed numbers can be used more than once, but not in the same pair.

Hint

First convert the fractions to equivalent fractions with the same denominator.

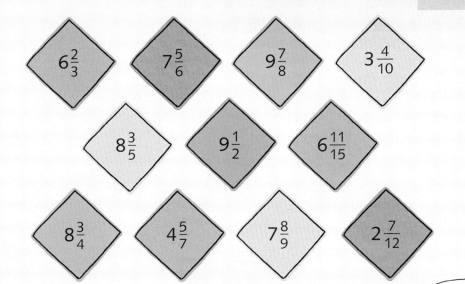

Example

$7\frac{2}{3} + 3\frac{7}{8}$

$7 + 3 = 10$

$\frac{2}{3} + \frac{7}{8} = \frac{16}{24} + \frac{21}{24}$

$= \frac{37}{24}$

$= 1\frac{13}{24}$

$10 + 1\frac{13}{24} = 11\frac{13}{24}$

3 Which combinations of mixed numbers in Question 2 did you find easiest to add? Explain why.

Check that your answers are simplified to the lowest form.

1 Add these improper fractions. Write each answer as a mixed number.

  a $\frac{5}{3} + \frac{4}{3}$ **b** $\frac{6}{8} + \frac{7}{8}$ **c** $\frac{9}{4} + \frac{5}{4}$ **d** $\frac{7}{5} + \frac{8}{5}$ **e** $\frac{3}{2} + \frac{5}{2}$

  f $\frac{9}{6} + \frac{7}{6}$ **g** $\frac{12}{10} + \frac{15}{10}$ **h** $\frac{11}{5} + \frac{9}{5}$ **i** $\frac{8}{4} + \frac{9}{4}$ **j** $\frac{15}{12} + \frac{14}{12}$

2 Choose three of the mixed numbers below and add them together. Do this five times. The mixed numbers can be used more than once.

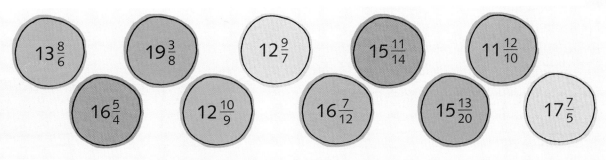

3 Which combinations of mixed numbers in Question 2 did you find easiest to add? Explain why.

Subtracting fractions

Subtract fractions with different denominators and mixed numbers, using the concept of equivalent fractions

1 Subtract these fractions. Change any answers that are improper fractions to mixed numbers.

Example

$$\frac{7}{4} - \frac{2}{4} = \frac{5}{4} = 1\frac{1}{4}$$

a $\frac{9}{5} - \frac{3}{5}$ **b** $\frac{10}{8} - \frac{4}{8}$ **c** $\frac{8}{6} - \frac{4}{6}$ **d** $\frac{12}{7} - \frac{3}{7}$ **e** $\frac{6}{4} - \frac{1}{4}$

f $\frac{5}{3} - \frac{2}{3}$ **g** $\frac{11}{9} - \frac{6}{9}$ **h** $\frac{3}{2} - \frac{2}{2}$ **i** $\frac{13}{8} - \frac{7}{8}$ **j** $\frac{14}{11} - \frac{8}{11}$

2 Subtract these mixed numbers. Show your working.

Example

$$5\frac{4}{6} - 2\frac{2}{6}$$

$$5 - 2 = 3$$

$$\frac{4}{6} - \frac{2}{6} = \frac{2}{6}$$

$$3 + \frac{2}{6} = 3\frac{2}{6} = 3\frac{1}{3}$$

a $7\frac{5}{8} - 2\frac{3}{8}$ **b** $5\frac{4}{7} - 2\frac{1}{7}$ **c** $8\frac{3}{4} - 3\frac{1}{4}$

d $7\frac{9}{10} - 6\frac{4}{10}$ **e** $9\frac{4}{5} - 2\frac{3}{5}$ **f** $7\frac{5}{6} - 3\frac{4}{6}$

g $8\frac{7}{9} - 4\frac{2}{9}$ **h** $4\frac{1}{2} - 2\frac{1}{2}$

i $7\frac{3}{12} - 5\frac{1}{12}$ **j** $9\frac{6}{10} - 9\frac{2}{10}$

Example

We can't subtract the fractions as $\frac{3}{5}$ is less than $\frac{4}{5}$. So, exchange 1 whole for 5 fifths. $4\frac{3}{5} = 3\frac{8}{5}$

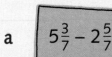

1 Subtract these mixed numbers. The first mixed number will need exchanging, as shown in the example.

$$4\frac{3}{5} - 2\frac{4}{5} = 3\frac{8}{5} - 2\frac{4}{5}$$

$$= 1\frac{4}{5}$$

a $5\frac{3}{7} - 2\frac{5}{7}$ **b** $8\frac{2}{5} - 3\frac{4}{5}$

c $7\frac{3}{8} - 4\frac{7}{8}$ **d** $9\frac{1}{6} - 5\frac{4}{6}$ **e** $7\frac{1}{3} - 4\frac{2}{3}$ **f** $10\frac{5}{9} - 4\frac{7}{9}$

g $12\frac{1}{4} - 8\frac{3}{4}$ **h** $15\frac{2}{6} - 11\frac{4}{6}$ **i** $10\frac{2}{12} - 5\frac{7}{12}$ **j** $11\frac{1}{8} - 3\frac{2}{8}$

2 Subtract these mixed numbers. First convert the fractions to equivalent fractions with the same denominator.

ge

a $\left(6\frac{3}{4} - 2\frac{2}{6}\right)$ b $\left(7\frac{2}{3} - 4\frac{1}{4}\right)$ c $\left(9\frac{4}{5} - 3\frac{4}{15}\right)$

d $\left(8\frac{6}{8} - 1\frac{3}{12}\right)$ e $\left(9\frac{8}{10} - 2\frac{3}{4}\right)$ f $\left(10\frac{6}{7} - 3\frac{1}{2}\right)$

g $\left(12\frac{7}{9} - 5\frac{2}{6}\right)$ h $\left(11\frac{3}{4} - 4\frac{2}{5}\right)$

i $\left(16\frac{6}{7} - 11\frac{1}{3}\right)$ j $\left(14\frac{8}{9} - 5\frac{3}{4}\right)$

Check your answers are in the simplest form.

Example

$7\frac{6}{8} - 5\frac{5}{12}$

$7 - 5 = 2$

$\frac{6}{8} - \frac{5}{12} = \frac{18}{24} - \frac{10}{24}$

$\phantom{\frac{6}{8} - \frac{5}{12}} = \frac{8}{24}$

$\phantom{\frac{6}{8} - \frac{5}{12}} = \frac{1}{3}$

$2 + \frac{1}{3} = 2\frac{1}{3}$

1 Look at the calculations in Question 2, below. Predict the calculations where the first mixed number will need exchanging, even after you have found the common denominator. Write the letters of these calculations in your book. Choose one of them and explain how you knew.

2 Work out these calculations.

a $11\frac{3}{5} - 3\frac{2}{10}$ b $9\frac{3}{4} - 5\frac{2}{5}$ c $13\frac{1}{6} - 7\frac{5}{9}$ d $15\frac{7}{10} - 8\frac{3}{15}$

e $12\frac{7}{12} - 4\frac{1}{2}$ f $16\frac{4}{7} - 10\frac{2}{3}$ g $21\frac{4}{5} - 17\frac{2}{6}$ h $19\frac{2}{6} - 12\frac{1}{7}$

i $20\frac{1}{2} - 14\frac{2}{5}$ j $21\frac{4}{5} - 8\frac{3}{9}$ k $16\frac{5}{8} - 13\frac{2}{3}$ l $22\frac{3}{5} - 18\frac{7}{15}$

3 Write a set of instructions for subtracting mixed numbers. Include instructions for when the fractions have different denominators and when the first fraction needs exchanging.

43

Using coordinates to locate shapes (I)

Use coordinates to describe positions in two and in four quadrants and predict missing coordinates

1 The points on the grid represent five footballers on a football pitch. Write the coordinates of players A to E.

2 The ball is at the point X (−2, 3).

Decide where to position the referee and write the coordinates as R (,). Explain your choice.

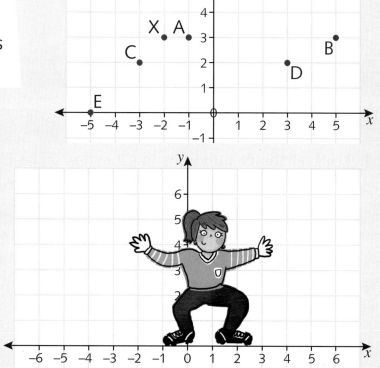

1 The Cup Final has gone to a penalty shoot-out.

- The shot is a miss if the goalkeeper covers the coordinates.

- The shot is a goal if the coordinates are not covered by the goalkeeper.

a Copy and complete the score sheet for each team.

Rustean Rovers					
Coordinates of shot	(−2, 4)	(−5, 6)	(3, 4)	(−4, 1)	(2, 2)
Result	miss				

Ashwell United					
Coordinates of shot	(3, 5)	(−6, 1)	(−1, 2)	(3, 4)	(−3, 3)
Result					

b Which team won the Cup?

2 List the coordinates of the vertices of each shape.

a square ABCD

b rectangle EFGH

c parallelogram KLMN

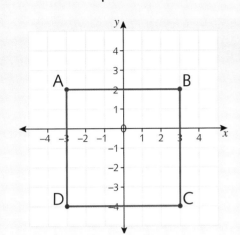 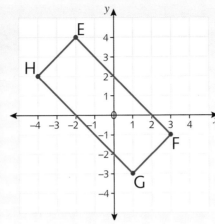 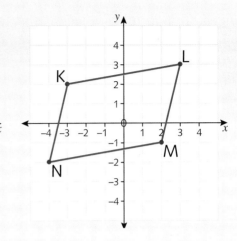

3 The points R, S and T form three of the vertices of a rhombus.

What are the coordinates of the fourth vertex U?

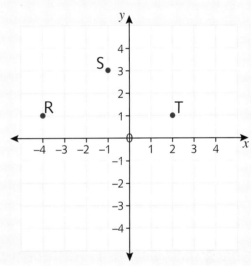

1 List the coordinates of the four points that are the vertices of:

a a square

b two parallelograms

c an isosceles triangle with all angles less than 90°.

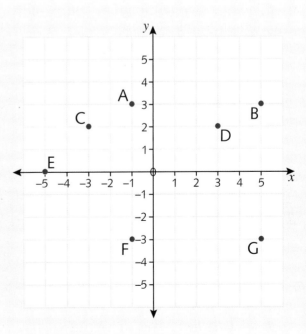

2 The points D (3, 2) and F (−1, −3) are two vertices of a scalene triangle. Find two different coordinates for the third vertex.

Plotting shapes in the four quadrants (1)

Plot, draw and label shapes in the four quadrants and predict missing coordinates

Challenge 1

Use Resource 12: 4-quadrant coordinate grids.

You will need:
- copies of Resource 12: 4-quadrant coordinate grids
- ruler

1 Plot these points on one of the grids.

A (4, 4)	B (−3, 3)
C (2, 3)	D (−5, 2)
E (−4, 0)	F (−3, −2)
G (2, −2)	H (0, −3)

2 Write the letter of the point or points that are:

  a in the 2nd quadrant   **b** in the 3rd quadrant

  c in the 4th quadrant   **d** on the x-axis   **e** on the y-axis

3 Using a ruler, join the points B, C, G and F in order to form a square.

Challenge 2

For each diagram, use a different grid on Resource 12: 4-quadrant coordinate grids.

1 On four separate grids, plot each point and join the points in order:

  a rectangle ABCD:
    A (−2, 3), B (3, 3),
    C (3, −4), D (−2, −4)

  b square EFGH:
    E (1, 3), F (5, −1),
    G (1, −5), H (−3, −1)

  c parallelogram IJKL:
    I (−3, 2), J (5, 2),
    K (3, −3), L (−5, −3)

  d rhombus PQRS:
    P (0, 0), Q (4, −2),
    R (0, −4), S (−4, −2)

2 The points T (−3, 3), U (3, 2) and V (2, −4) are three vertices of a square.

- Plot the points and join them in order, T to U and U to V.

- Find the coordinates of the missing vertex W.

- Complete the drawing of the square.

3 The points A (–5, –1), B (1, 5) and C (5, 1)
are three vertices of a rectangle.

- Plot the points and join them in order, A to B and B to C.

- Find the coordinates of the missing vertex D.

- Complete the drawing of the rectangle.

4 The points E (3, 4), F (3, –3) and G (–3, –5)
are three vertices of a parallelogram.

- Plot the points and join them in order, E to F and F to G.

- Find the coordinates of the missing vertex H.

- Complete the drawing of the parallelogram.

5 The points J (–1, 3), K (1, 0) and L (–1, –3)
are three vertices of a rhombus.

- Plot the points and join them in order, J to K and K to L.

- Find the coordinates of the missing vertex M.

- Complete the drawing of the rhombus.

For each diagram, use a different grid on Resource 12:
4-quadrant coordinate grids.

1 AB is one side of a square ABCD, with A (0, –1) and B (4, –1).

- Plot the points A and B.

- Find two sets of coordinates for the missing vertices C and D.

- Complete the drawings of the squares.

2 FH is a diagonal of a square EFGH, with F (2, 3) and H (–4, –3).

- Plot the points F and H.

- Find the coordinates for the missing vertices E and G.

- Complete the drawing of the square.

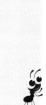

Using coordinates to translate shapes (1)

Use coordinates to translate shapes into all four quadrants

Challenge 1

For each grid, write the translation of shape A to shape B.

Example

2 squares left, 3 squares down

Grid 1

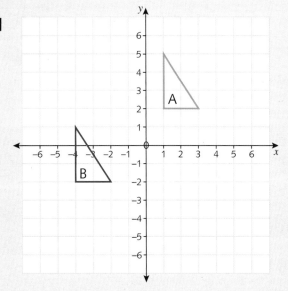

Grid 2

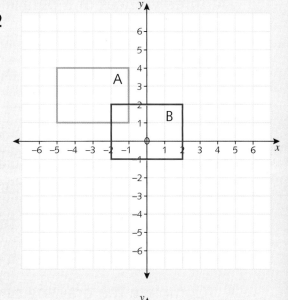

Grid 3

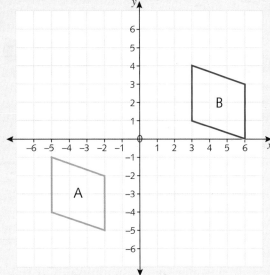

Grid 4

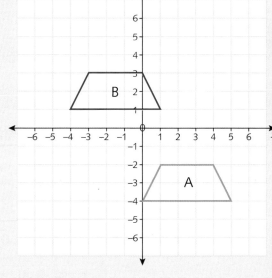

Challenge 2

1 Copy each green shape A in Grids 1 to 4 of Challenge 1 onto four different grids on Resource 12: 4-quadrant coordinate grids.

You will need:

- copies of Resource 12: 4-quadrant coordinate grids
- ruler
- green coloured pencil

For each one, translate shape A, as described below, to form shape B.

- **Grid 1:** 2 squares left, 3 squares down
- **Grid 2:** 6 squares right, 2 squares down
- **Grid 3:** 4 squares right, 3 squares up
- **Grid 4:** 1 square left, 6 squares up

2 Copy shapes A, B and C onto a grid on Resource 12: 4-quadrant coordinate grids.

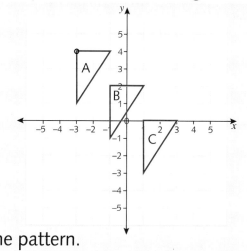

Shape	x-coordinate	y-coordinate
A	−3	4
B	−1	2
C	1	0
D		

- The table shows the coordinates for the corresponding vertices for shapes A, B and C. Copy and complete the table giving the corresponding vertex for shape D by following the pattern.
- Draw shape D on the grid.

3 Copy the shapes D, E and F onto a grid on Resource 12: 4-quadrant coordinate grids.

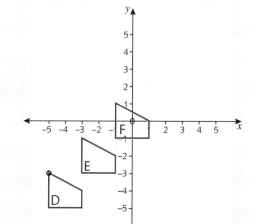

Shape	x-coordinate	y-coordinate
D	−5	−3
E		
F		
G		

- Copy the table and fill in the corresponding vertices for shapes E and F.
- Work out and record the corresponding vertex for shape G by following the pattern.
- Draw shape G on the grid.

1 Design a different translating pattern for the trapezium in Challenge 2, Question 3 and draw three translations of the shape on a grid on Resource 12: 4-quadrant coordinate grids.

2 Choose a corresponding vertex for each shape and write their coordinates in a table.

3 Draw the next translation of the shape on the grid.

You will need:
- Resource 12: 4-quadrant coordinate grids
- ruler

Using coordinates to reflect shapes

Use coordinates to reflect shapes into all four quadrants

1 Write the coordinates of each point and its image when reflected in the y-axis.

You will need:
- Resource 13: 2-quadrant coordinate grids
- ruler

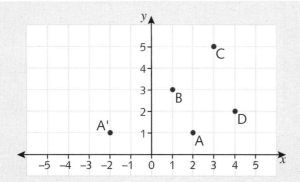

Example

A (2, 1)   A' (−2, 1)

2 Copy each shape onto a different grid on Resource 13: 2-quadrant coordinate grids. Reflect each shape in the y-axis.

a

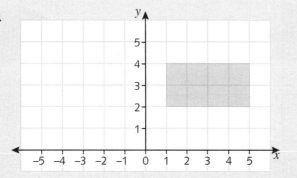

b

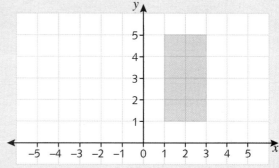

1 Write the coordinates of each point and its image when reflected in the x-axis.

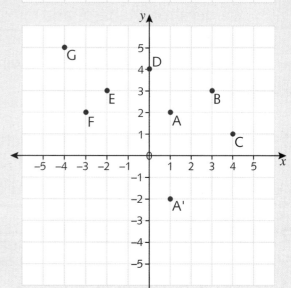

Example

A (1, 2)   A' (1, −2)

2 Copy each shape from the grids below onto a different grid on Resource 12: 4-quadrant coordinate grids.

For both Grids 1 and 2, draw the reflection of the shape in the y-axis and in the x-axis and write the coordinates for the vertices and their images.

You will need:
- Resource 12: 4-quadrant coordinate grids
- ruler

Grid 1

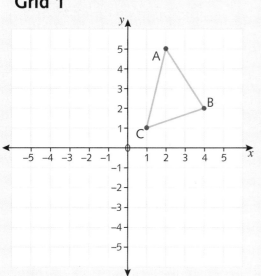

Grid 2

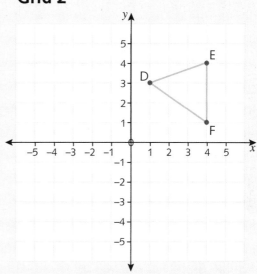

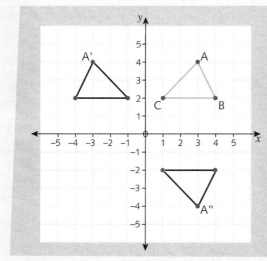

Example

A (3, 4), A' (−3, 4), A" (3, −4)

B (4, 2), B' (−4, 2), B" (4, −2)

C (1, 2), C'(−1, 2), C"(1, −2)

Draw a triangle with vertices P (0, 2), Q (4, 5) and R (3, 1) on Resource 12: 4-quadrant coordinate grids.

You will need:
- Resource 12: 4-quadrant coordinate grids
- ruler

a Reflect the triangle in the y-axis and write the coordinates of P', Q' and R'.

b Reflect the triangle in the x-axis and write the coordinates of P", Q" and R".

Written addition

- Add whole numbers using the formal written method of columnar addition
- Estimate and check the answer to a calculation

Challenge 1

Estimate the answer to each calculation, then work it out.

a 362,185 + 153,704   b 415,721 + 347,534

c 561,942 + 473,248   d 628,653 + 306,729

e 525,285 + 247,907   f 274,924 + 586,058

g 483,517 + 494,725   h 638,364 + 257,851

i 296,342 + 631,729   j 472,348 + 529,885

Example

361,258 + 636,581
→ 360,000 + 640,000 = 1,000,0

```
   361258
+  636581
   997839
        1
```

Challenge 2

1 Estimate the answer to each calculation, then work it out.

a 3,762,485 + 1,229,152   b 2,383,962 + 2,652,725

c 4,296,422 + 3,487,384   d 2,762,471 + 4,083,982

e 4,282,692 + 3,815,854   f 6,385,352 + 2,563,983

g 3,592,284 + 5,835,799   h 5,836,365 + 3,927,289

i 2,973,483 + 605,863   j 716,493 + 3,853,632

k 67,892 + 1,360,542   l 4,396,387 + 728,195

m 6,396,293 + 45,829   n 768,219 + 6,926,103

2 Using the digit cards, make two 7-digit numbers so that when added together the sum is the largest possible number. The digits in each column must be different. Use trial and improvement to get the largest answer you can.

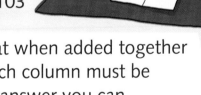

3 Using the same digits, make the smallest possible answer. Remember to use trial and improvement.

1 Estimate the answer to each calculation, then work it out.

a 6,734 + 742,984 + 2,386,281

b 34,825 + 4,254,106 + 3,762

c 23,876 + 58,108 + 2,782,354

d 5,387,205 + 38,298 + 599,486

e 3,293,382 + 617,296 + 4,286,125

f 687,462 + 836,277 + 4,275,196

g 383,582 + 9,607,306 + 1,933

h 61,012 + 426,719 + 2,808,911

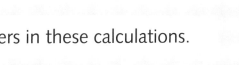

Example

2,365,256 + 851,734 + 65,726
→ 2,000,000 + 900,000 + 70,000 = 2,970,000

```
  2365256
   851734
+    65726
  3282716
  ‾‾‾‾‾‾‾
  1 1 1 1 1 1
```

2 Work out the missing numbers in these calculations.

a 3,872,386 + _____ = 5,803,862

b 872,492 + _____ = 2,764,821

c 3,297,378 + _____ = 5,545,503

d 2,764,297 + _____ = 4,723,285

e 876,955 + _____ = 3,608,275

f 75,316 + 483,592 + _____ = 2,685,273

g 650,732 + 1,487,284 + _____ = 4,217,639

h 782,916 + 2,935,272 + _____ = 5,074,286

i 615,109 + _____ + 1,696,500 = 9,809,205

j 974,486 + _____ + 40,792 = 3,084,817

Written subtraction

- Subtract whole numbers using the formal written method of columnar subtraction
- Estimate and check the answer to a calculation

Estimate the answer to each calculation, then work it out.

a   573,296 – 281,542   b   427,386 – 193,228

c   632,492 – 307,915   d   426,145 – 281,630

e   574,851 – 327,188   f   803,274 – 351,748

g   956,062 – 672,391   h   944,264 – 587,093

i   893,216 – 775,608   j   816,749 – 652,871

1 Estimate the answer to each calculation, then work it out.

Example
$$2,636,581 – 361,258$$
$$\rightarrow 2,600,000 – 400,000 = 2,200,000$$

```
      5 13     7 11
    2 6̸ 3̸ 6 5 8 1̸
  –   3 6 1 2 5 8
    ─────────────
    2 2 7 5 3 2 3
```

a   5,487,287 – 3,429,159

b   4,252,961 – 2,504,315

c   7,289,242 – 3,739,625

d   6,029,882 – 2,415,945   e   9,401,194 – 4,721,638

f   8,339,327 – 1,728,543   g   7,284,191 – 5,471,654

h   9,386,194 – 5,847,528   i   4,296,252 – 735,298

j   5,825,261 – 563,865   k   638,194 – 8,369

l   3,296,285 – 9,673   m   2,384,901 – 863,552

n   836,285 – 89,644   o   7,291,304 – 862,899

p   6,928,362 – 725,633   q   8,296,235 – 9,727

r   9,007,296 – 451,167

2 Look at the following set of subtraction calculations. Think carefully about how you are going to use the formal written method of subtraction to work out the answers to these calculations.

    a 5,872,130 – 2,874,274 – 674,923

    b 7,394,866 – 538,744 – 2,651,908

    c 6,458,428 – 2,649,106 – 9,533

    d 4,936,282 – 3,371,627 – 1,386,395

    e 7,635,863 – 2,863,364 – 3,654,399

    f 8,362,392 – 584,274 – 4,722,564

    g 7,100,285 – 1,783,551 – 741,302

    h 3,651,299 – 376,297 – 486,555

    i 9,715,351 – 4,726,337 – 3,075,283

    j 8,247,561 – 9,999 – 3,762,286

nge

Work out the missing numbers in these calculations.

    a 6,397,282 –   = 4,276,295

    b 5,207,466 –   = 1,542,396

    c 4,296,385 –   = 2,524,719

    d 3,829,603 –   = 2,657,843

    e 8,602,552 –   = 864,971

    f   – 2,864,296 = 4,872,381

    g   – 378,272 = 3,981,228

    h   – 1,872,398 = 4,882,396

    i   – 9,762 = 8,376,281

    j   – 801,362 = 7,449,276

Adding and subtracting decimals (2)

- Add and subtract decimals using the formal written methods of columnar addition and subtraction
- Estimate and check the answer to a calculation

Challenge 1

Work out these calculations.

a	3,874·48 + 4,153·35	**b**	5,247·27 + 3,164·43
c	2,914·56 + 4,253·21	**d**	3,225·37 + 2,834·91
e	7,625·28 – 3,714·16	**f**	8,364·36 – 5,295·29
g	6,268·65 – 2,173·72	**h**	9,467·78 – 5,831·95

Example

6,581·57 + 1,258·44

→ 6,600 + 1,200 = 7,800

```
  6581·57
+ 1258·44
─────────
  7840·01
   1 11  1
```

Challenge 2

1 Work out these calculations.

a	63,326·58 + 31,461·71	**b**	52,461·62 + 43,315·53
c	61,352·48 + 27,632·92	**d**	83,479·24 + 15,380·93
e	48,252·64 + 37,463·78	**f**	59,361·72 + 63,482·52
g	86,452·83 – 59,261·91	**h**	74,375·03 – 25,614·65

Example

8,076·19 – 5,456·42

→ 8,100 – 5,500 = 2,600

```
  7 10 6 15 11
  8 0 7 6 · 1 9
– 5 4 5 6 · 4 2
───────────────
  2 6 1 9 · 7 7
```

2 Play this addition game in a group of 2–4 players.

- Each player shuffles their cards and lays out ten each.
- Then, using the decimal point cards, players place their cards in this arrangement:

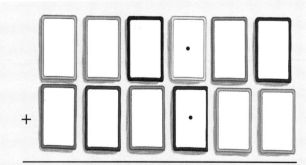

You will need:
- two sets 0–9 digit cards per player
- three decimal point cards per player
- pencil
- paper
- about 20 counters per group

- Players then work out the answer to their calculation.
- The winner of each round is the player with the largest total, and that player collects a counter.
- The overall winner is the player with most counters after six rounds.

3 Play this subtraction game in a group of 2–4 players.

- Each player shuffles their cards and lays out ten each.
- Then, using their the decimal point cards, players place their cards in this arrangement:

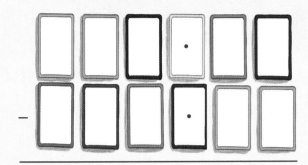 

- Players then work out the answer to their calculation.
- The winner of each round is the player with the smallest answer, and that player collects a counter.
- The overall winner is the player with most counters after six rounds.

1 Work out these calculations.

a 2,487·46 + 27,826·3   b 45,272·72 – 3,962·8

c 52,835·35 + 286,486·62   d 731,362·5 + 67,251·2

e 65,972·98 – 42,252·382   f 82,616·3 – 5,826·296

2 These numbers are the answers. Write one addition and one subtraction calculation for each answer. The calculations must be 8-digit to 2 decimal places plus/minus 8-digit to 2 decimal places.

> **Hint**
>
> Use the inverse operation!

a 462,712·53   b 504,724·62   c 826,507·11

d 483,566·72   e 638,931·63   f 847,116·83

Book problems

- Solve multi-step problems, deciding which operations and methods to use and why
- Estimate and check the answer to a calculation

The tables below show the bestselling books of all time.

Bestselling books 1–10		
Position	Type of book	Total sales
1st	mystery novel	5,094,805
2nd	children's	4,475,152
3rd	children's	4,200,654
4th	children's	4,179,479
5th	novel	3,758,936
6th	children's	3,583,215
7th	children's	3,484,047
8th	children's	3,377,906
9th	mystery novel	3,193,346
10th	children's	2,950,264

Bestselling books 90–100		
Position	Type of book	Total sales
90th	science	816,907
91st	comic annual	816,585
92nd	novel	815,586
93rd	novel	814,370
94th	novel	809,641
95th	novel	808,311
96th	novel	807,311
97th	cookery	794,201
98th	novel	792,187
99th	autobiography	791,507
100th	cookery	791,095

Challenge 1

Answer these problems.

a What is the difference in sales between the 92nd most popular book and the 97th most popular book?

b What are the total sales for both cookery books?

c Josh buys a cookery book and a novel. He pays £38. Salma buys the same cookery book and two copies of the same novel as Josh. She pays £45. What is the price of the cookery book?

d If the autobiography sells a further 32,000 copies in shops and 43,000 copies online, what would be the total sales?

Answer these problems.

a The total sales for the top two bestselling children's books is 8,675,806. The total sales for hardback books was 3,400,000. Book One sold 2,500,000 copies in hardback. Book Two sold 3,300,654 copies in paperback. How many copies of Book Two were sold in hardback? How many copies of Book One were sold in paperback?

b The price of the bestselling children's novel was £7 at the local shop. A bookshop allocated £8,450 to spend on copies of the novel. They ordered as many copies as they could afford. How much money was left over?

c Josh rounds the sales of two of the books and adds them together. His answer is 1,618,000. Which two books' sales did he round?

d Salma finds the difference between the sales of two books from the top ten. Her answer was 381,030. Which two books did she choose?

1 Answer these problems.

a Three friends go into the bookshop. Billy buys a mystery novel and a science book. He pays £19.94. Gemma buys the same science book and an atlas. Her bill comes to £28.98. Louis buys the mystery novel and the atlas and pays £24.94. What is the price of each book?

b The publisher ordered more copies of its two bestsellers, a novel and a cookery book, to be printed. The novel was packed in crates of 10,000 and the cookery book, as it was larger, was packed in crates of 3,000.

If 210,000 copies of each book were printed, how many more crates of cookery books were there than novels?

c What were the total sales of the three most popular children's books?

d The author of the bestselling detective novel signed approximately 12,700 copies of his book. The author of the bestselling children's book managed to sign more of her books, and 4,461,152 copies were sold unsigned. What was the total number of signed books sold?

2 Write a challenging word problem using the information in the table and give it to your partner to work out.

Numbers with 3 decimal places

Identify the value of each digit in a number with 3 decimal places

Challenge 1

1 Count on five numbers from each number with 2 decimal places.

Example

6·38 , 6·39, 6·4, 6·41, 6·42, 6·43

a 3·47 b 2·89 c 4·07 d 5·26 e 3·98 f 4·57

g 6·39 h 2·06 i 8·18 j 4·95 k 7·35 l 8·88

2 Look at the decimal numbers in Question 1. What two numbers with 1 decimal place do they come between?

Example

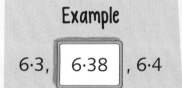

6·3, 6·38 , 6·4

Hint
Convert the tenths into hundredths,
6·3 to 6·30 and 6·4 to 6·40.

Challenge 2

1 Count on five numbers from each number with 3 decimal places.

Example

6·328 , 6·329, 6·330, 6·331, 6·332, 6·333

a 3·867 b 6·108 c 2·759 d 9·015 e 4·268 f 7·009

g 5·486 h 3·111 i 5·437 j 6·546 k 1·001 l 4·873

2 Look at the decimal numbers in Question 1. What two numbers with 2 decimal places do they come between?

Example

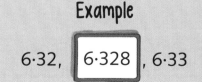

6·32, 6·328 , 6·33

Hint
Convert the hundredths into thousandths,
6·32 to 6·320 and 6·33 to 6·330.

3 Choose five numbers from Question 1 and write the value of each of the digits.

Example

$6·328 = 6 + 0·3 + 0·02 + 0·008$

4 Put all the numbers from Question 1 in order, smallest to largest.

5 Write ten numbers with 3 decimal places where:

- the thousandths digit is even
- the hundredths digit is less than 5
- the tenths digit is half the thousandths digit.

3·428 fits all these properties.

1 Use these four digit cards.

5   9   2   7

a Make twelve different numbers with a 1s digit and 3 decimal places.

b Write the numbers in order, smallest to largest, leaving a space in between each of the numbers.

Example

2·579, ⬚ , 2·597, ⬚ , 5·279 …

c Write numbers with 3 decimal places that could lie between your numbers and keep the order.

2 Write a number with 3 decimal places that could lie between each pair of decimals.

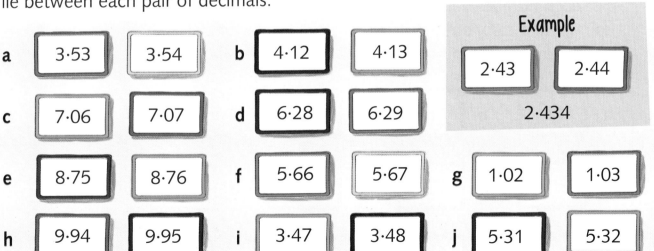

a 3·53	3·54	**b** 4·12	4·13		

Example

2·43   2·44

2·434

c 7·06	7·07	**d** 6·28	6·29		
e 8·75	8·76	**f** 5·66	5·67	**g** 1·02	1·03
h 9·94	9·95	**i** 3·47	3·48	**j** 5·31	5·32

Multiplying and dividing by 10, 100 and 1,000

Multiply and divide numbers by 10, 100 and 1,000 where the answers are up to 3 decimal places

Challenge 1

1 Use Resource 15: 10, 100 spinner. For each number below, spin the spinner and carry out the operation it lands on.

You will need:
- Resource 15: 10, 100 spinner
- paper clip and pencil – for the spinner

	a	b	c	d
	28	150	63	89
e	580	f 630	g 72	h 370
i	230	j 487	k 362	l 163

Example
52
52 × 10 = 520
or
52 × 100 = 5,200
or
52 ÷ 10 = 5·2
or
52 ÷ 100 = 0·52

2 Explain what happens when a number is multiplied by 100.

3 Explain what happens when a number is divided by 10.

Challenge 2

1 Use Resource 34: ÷ 10, ÷ 100, ÷ 1,000, × 10, × 100, × 1,000 spinner. For each number below, spin the spinner and carry out the operation it lands on.

You will need:
- Resource 34: ÷ 10, ÷ 100, ÷ 1,000, × 10, × 100, × 1,000 spinner.
- paper clip and pencil – for the spinner

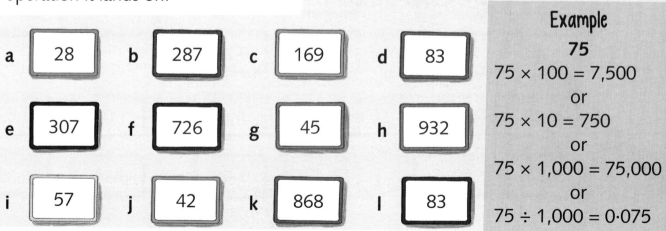

a	b	c	d
28	287	169	83
e 307	f 726	g 45	h 932
i 57	j 42	k 868	l 83

Example
75
75 × 100 = 7,500
or
75 × 10 = 750
or
75 × 1,000 = 75,000
or
75 ÷ 1,000 = 0·075

2 Multiply and divide each decimal number by 100.

a	36·2	**b**	83·6	**c**	92·5
d	73·1	**e**	43·7	**f**	63·2
g	92·9	**h**	28·3	**i**	82·7

Example

46·8

46·8 × 100 = 4,680

46·8 ÷ 100 = 0·468

3 Play this game with a partner. Use Resource 34.

- Choose a 2-digit start number and both write it down.
- Take turns to spin the spinner.
- Carry out the operation it lands on with your start number.
- Write your answer underneath your start number. This answer becomes your new start number.
- The winner is the player with the larger number after ten turns each.

1 Use Resource 34.
For each number, spin the spinner and carry out the operation it lands on.

You will need:
- Resource 34: ÷ 10, ÷ 100, ÷ 1,000, × 10, × 100, × 1,000 spinner
- paper clip and pencil – for the spinner

a 1,836	**b** 2,924		
c 3,715	**d** 5,206		
e 7,188	**f** 34,492	**g** 87,725	**h** 21,396
i 50,532	**j** 47,872	**k** 19,294	**l** 74,816

Example

25,486

25,486 × 1,000 = 25,486,000

25,486 ÷ 1,000 = 25·486

2 A supermarket orders different items in boxes of 100. They have just received the delivery below. How many of each item do they have?

- 36 boxes of dog food
- 260 boxes of cereal
- 198 boxes of biscuits
- 86·5 boxes of jam
  (One box got dropped on the way and half the jars were broken!)

3 Using Resource 34, work with a partner to design a game to practise multiplying and dividing by 10, 100 and 1,000.

Multiplying decimals

Multiply decimals by whole numbers including in practical contexts

Challenge 1

1 Copy and complete these decimal 'times tables'.

a	b	c
1 × 0·2 = 0·2	1 × 0·3 = 0·3	1 × 0·5 = 0·5
2 × 0·2 = 0·4	2 × 0·3 = 0·6	2 × 0·5 = 1
3 × 0·2 = 0·6	3 × 0·3 = 0·9	3 × 0·5 = 1·5
4 × 0·2 = 0·8	4 × 0·3 = 1·2	4 × 0·5 = 2
5 × 0·2 =	5 × 0·3 =	5 × 0·5 =
6 × 0·2 =	6 × 0·3 =	6 × 0·5 =
7 × 0·2 =	7 × 0·3 =	7 × 0·5 =
8 × 0·2 =	8 × 0·3 =	8 × 0·5 =
9 × 0·2 =	9 × 0·3 =	9 × 0·5 =
10 × 0·2 =	10 × 0·3 =	10 × 0·5 =
11 × 0·2 =	11 × 0·3 =	11 × 0·5 =
12 × 0·2 =	12 × 0·3 =	12 × 0·5 =

2 Work out each calculation. In brackets, write the times table fact that helps you work it out.

Example

0·4 × 3 = 1·2 (4 × 3 = 12)

a 0·4 × 2

b 0·4 × 5

c 0·6 × 2

d 0·6 × 4

e 0·7 × 5

f 0·8 × 3

Challenge 2

1 Copy and complete these decimal 'times tables'.

1 × 0·6 = 0·6	2 × 0·6 = 1·2	3 × 0·6 =
4 × 0·6 =	5 × 0·6 =	6 × 0·6 =
7 × 0·6 =	8 × 0·6 =	9 × 0·6 =
10 × 0·6 =	11 × 0·6 =	12 × 0·6 =

2 Which 'decimal × whole number' calculations will these multiplication facts help you work out?

Example
Multiplication fact: 3 × 4 = 12
0·3 × 4 = 1·2
3 × 0·4 = 1·2

a 5 × 3	**b** 4 × 7	**c** 2 × 8	**d** 6 × 3	**e** 8 × 4
f 7 × 6	**g** 3 × 9	**h** 5 × 6	**i** 8 × 9	**j** 7 × 7

3 Work out the cost of these items. Show your working.

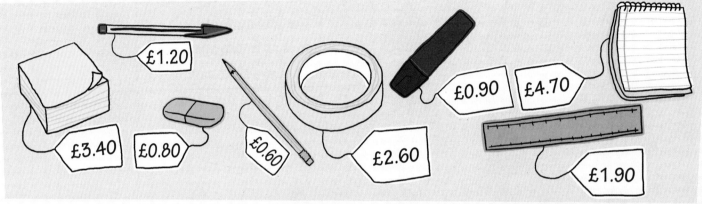

a 6 pencils	**b** 8 erasers	**c** 13 highlighter pens
d 4 sticky note pads	**e** 7 rulers	**f** 15 pens and 7 erasers
g 12 rolls of sticky tape	**h** 5 notebooks	**i** 13 rulers and 20 pencils

1 Copy and complete this bill from the hardware shop.

Item	Price per metre	Number of metres	Calculation	Total price
string	£0.70	24		
rope	£0.90	31		
leather	£4	15·6		
fine wire	£2.30	27		
nylon rope	£0.40	43		
thick wire	£2.70	35		
chain	£3.20	40		

2 Stan goes to the hardware shop. He has £20 to spend.
How many metres of string can he buy? How much change will he get?

3 William has £30 to spend. He wants to buy a combination of rope and fine wire. He needs more rope than wire. He wants to spend as much of his money as he can. What should he buy?

Rounding decimals

Solve problems which require answers to be rounded to specified degrees of accuracy

Challenge 1

1 Round these decimals to the nearest whole number.

a 4·6   b 2·8   c 7·3

If the tenths digit is less than 5, the ones digit stays the same. If the tenths digit is 5 or greater, round up the ones digit.

d 9·5   e 1·4   f 3·6

g 8·8   h 3·2   i 8·4

j 5·1   k 8·8   l 9·1   m 7·5   n 2·6

2 Write five decimal numbers that would round to each of these numbers.

a 5   b 7   c 3   d 4   e 10

Challenge 2

1 Round these decimals to the nearest whole number.

Example
36·7 rounds to 37
35·79 rounds to 36

a 35·7   b 28·62   c 49·5   d 26·32

e 41·74   f 50·4   g 18·61   h 63·49   i 28·17

j 83·1   k 47·39   l 72·88   m 17·99   n 56·5

2 Round all the numbers with 2 decimal places from Question 1 to the nearest tenth.

3 Write five decimals that would round to each of these tenths.

a 6·2   b 2·9   c 1·4   d 5·7   e 9·1   f 3·6

4 For each of these measurements, write down a time when:

- the exact measurement would be best
- the measurement rounded to the nearest tenth would be best
- the measurement rounded to the nearest whole number would be best.

Explain your reasoning.

a Sophie is 1·45 metres tall.

b The hall is 35·82 metres long.

c A book costs £4.85.

d The recipe says '0·75 kg of flour'.

e The tree is 11·25 metres tall.

f The distance from home to school is 4·37 km.

g The dog weighs 6·98 kg.

h The play lasts 2·5 hours.

1 Round these decimals to the nearest whole number.

a 37·963	**b** 26·286	**c** 39·301	**d** 48·199	**e** 93·832
f 25·726	**g** 49·075	**h** 35·542	**i** 95·478	**j** 86·501
k 68·383	**l** 74·307	**m** 49·968	**n** 56·535	**o** 27·455

2 Choose five decimals from Question 1 and round each number to the nearest tenth.

3 Choose five different decimals from Question 1 and round each number to the nearest hundredth.

4 Jemima says, "When I go to the supermarket, I estimate my total bill this way: whenever I put anything in the trolley, I round it to the nearest pound."

a Write a shopping bill with prices of ten items where her system would work.

b Write another shopping bill with prices of ten items where it would not work.

c Overall, do you think Jemima's system is a good one? Explain your reasoning.

Converting units of length

Convert from smaller to larger units of length using decimal notation

Challenge 1

1 Write each length in centimetres using decimals.

  a 6 cm 3 mm   **b** 12 cm 9 mm   **c** 75 mm   **d** 148 mm

2 Write each length in metres using decimals.

  a 14 m 39 cm   **b** 52 m 60 cm   **c** 827 cm   **d** 309 cm

3 Write each length in kilometres using decimals.

  a 8 km 600 m   **b** 4 km 130 m   **c** 6,500 m   **d** 7,720 m

Challenge 2

1 Write each length in kilometres.

  a 3,727 m   **b** 4,420 m   **c** 5,010 m   **d** 3,205 m

2 Write each length in metres.

  a 0·725 km   **b** 0·408 km   **c** 914 cm   **d** 702 cm

3 Write each length in centimetres then order the lengths, longest to shortest.

  a 66 mm   **b** 242 mm   **c** 1·6 m   **d** 9·73 m

4 The carpenter has cut some strips of wood.

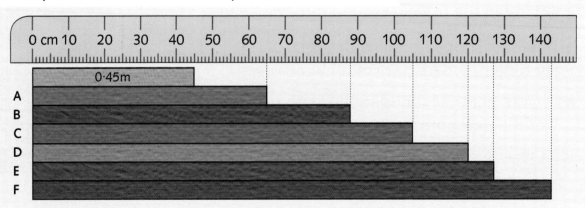

a Write the length of each strip of wood in metres.

b Work out the difference in length in centimetres between these strips of wood.

    i   A and D   **ii**   B and E   **iii**   C and F

c Work out the total length in metres of these strips of wood.

    i   A and E   **ii**   B and F   **iii**   C and B   **iv**   D and F

d How many metres long is each small piece of wood when:

    i   strip C is cut into 5 equal lengths?

    ii   strip D is cut into 8 equal lengths?

You have paving stones that are 1 m long and 0·5 m wide. How many different arrangements of paving stones can you make for 1 m wide paths that are 2 m, 2·5 m and 3 m long? Begin as shown in the Example.

You will need:
- 1 cm square dot paper

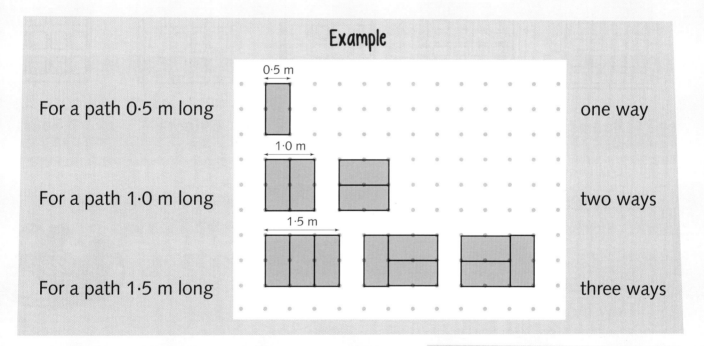

Example

For a path 0·5 m long	0·5 m	one way
For a path 1·0 m long	1·0 m	two ways
For a path 1·5 m long	1·5 m	three ways

a Draw the paths on 1 cm square dot paper until you see a pattern.

b Write in words how the pattern works.

Hint
The answer for a path 2·0 m long is not four ways!

c If the path was 5 m long, how many different arrangements of paving stones could you make? Investigate.

Sporting distances

Convert between units of length to solve problems using decimal notation

1 The cricket ground is overlooked by five blocks of flats. Work out the height of each block of flats.

Example

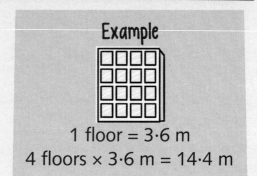

1 floor = 3·6 m
4 floors × 3·6 m = 14·4 m

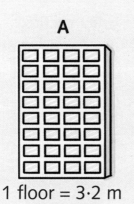

A

1 floor = 3·2 m
8 floors

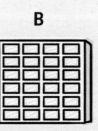

B

1 floor = 2·8 m
6 floors

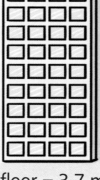

C

1 floor = 3·7 m
9 floors

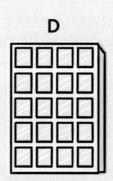

D

1 floor = 3·9 m
5 floors

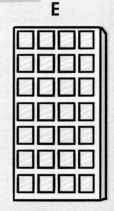

E

1 floor = 3·8 m
7 floors

2 How many metres taller is block C than:

   a block B?   **b** block D?

1 The distance round the sports ground running track is 420 m.
Colin runs nine times round the track in training.
How far does he run in kilometres?

2 Winston is a distance runner and he runs the same route every time.
In five evenings, he ran a total of 4·73 km. How long is his training route:

   a in kilometres?   **b** in metres?

3 Meg cycles 37·5 km from home to school and home again in one week.
How far is her house from her school?

4 The table shows the results of a long jump competition. By how many centimetres did Jordan beat each of his competitors?

Name	Jordan	Keira	Len	Mark	Naomi
Length of jump (m)	4·42	3·97	4·29	3·88	4·16

5 A cross-country cycle competition has races at six different venues in Britain. Work out the total length of each race in kilometres.

	Venue	Length of one course lap (km)	Number of laps
a	Peak District	3·87	4
b	Borders	2·85	5
c	Lake District	4·19	4
d	North Wales	5·025	3
e	South Downs	2·64	5
f	East Anglia	3·78	4

Sheena has to cut lengths of ribbon from a 32 m roll for the medals that the winners will receive at the school's sports day. She has mislaid her measuring tape and does the following:

- unrolls the ribbon, folds it in half and cuts it
- folds each piece in half and cuts it
- folds each of the four pieces in half and cuts them.

a How many pieces of ribbon will she have if she continues to fold and cut the ribbon a further three times?

b What is the final length of each piece of ribbon?

Hint
Making a table similar to this one will help organise your answer.

Number of folds	0	1	2	3
Number of pieces of ribbon	1	2	4	
Length of each piece of ribbon (m)	32	16	8	

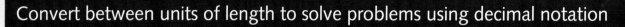

The Kelly family go to the circus

Convert between units of length to solve problems using decimal notation

This photograph of the Kelly children is for Gran. Alex wrote each of their heights underneath the photo so that Gran could see how tall they all were.

Alex 1·51 m Bob 1·25 m Chris 1·39 m Derek 1·44 m Ellen 96 cm

1 Work out, in metres, the difference in height between:

a Alex and Bob

b Alex and Chris

c Alex and Derek

d Alex and Ellen

2 Work out, in centimetres, the difference between the tallest and the shortest child.

3 Who is 14 cm taller than Bob?

1 The Kelly family have tickets for the circus in town. They travel 4·375 km by car to the station 'Park and Ride', 36·83 km by train to town and walk 50 m to the circus.

a How many kilometres do they travel altogether by car, there and back?

b How many kilometres is the round trip to and from the circus?

2 The tightrope wire is 21 m from the ground. The rungs on the ladder from the ground to the tightrope platform are at 60 cm intervals. Angelino, the tightrope walker, has climbed to the 15th rung from the ground.

a What is his height from the ground in metres?

b How many metres has he still to climb to reach the tightrope platform?

3 Chris Kelly's footprint is 245 mm long. The clown who wears enormous shoes has a footprint 8 times as long. Work out the length of the clown's footprint:

    a in centimetres   **b** in metres

4 The clown makes his own shoelaces.
Each lace is 85 cm long.

    a How many pairs of shoelaces can he make from a 10 m narrow strip of leather?

    b How many centimetres of leather will be left over?

5 Enrico needs some rope to tether the horses. He finds three lengths of rope in each of two boxes. If Enrico takes a length of rope from box A and joins it to one from box B, how many different lengths of combined rope can he make?

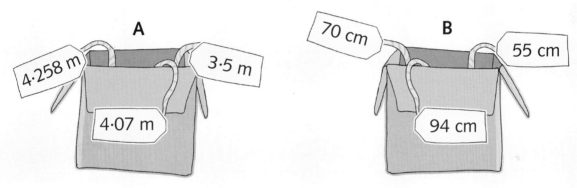

A: 4·258 m, 3·5 m, 4·07 m
B: 70 cm, 55 cm, 94 cm

The circus clowns have to ring the bell on top of each box, starting from one end of the double row of boxes, and visiting each bell once only. The clowns may not take any diagonal paths between the bells. The plan shows the distance between each bell.

a Work out the shortest route that a clown could take to ring all the bells.

b Write this shortest distance in metres.

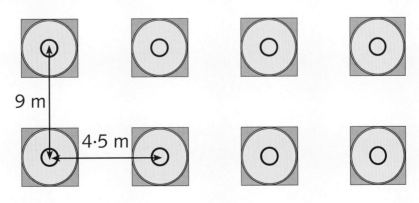

9 m   4·5 m

Converting miles to kilometres

Convert between miles and kilometres

You will need:
- Resource 17: Miles to kilometres conversion graph
- ruler

Challenges 1,2

1 Using the rule, copy and complete the table by converting miles to kilometres and using the distances to write the coordinates.

Rule
5 miles is approximately equal to 8 kilometres.

Miles	0	5	10	15	20	25
Kilometres	0	8				
Coordinates	(0, 0)	(5, 8)				

2 Use Resource 17: Miles to kilometres conversion graph.

- Plot the points from your table.
- Join the points with a ruler and a sharp pencil.
- Extend the straight line as far as it will go.

3 Use your graph from Question 2 to answer these questions.

a 16 km ≈ ⬚ miles

b 40 km ≈ ⬚ miles

≈ means 'approximately equal to'

c 15 miles ≈ ⬚ km

d 30 miles ≈ ⬚ km

Challenge 2

1 Use your graph from Challenge 1, Question 2 to convert these distances.

a 20 miles	b 35 miles	c 64 km
d 80 km	e 50 miles	f 60 miles

2 At point **a** on the straight line, 12 km converts to 7·5 miles.

Copy and complete for these points shown on the line.

Point	Kilometres	Miles
a	12	7·5
b	20	
c		
d		
e		

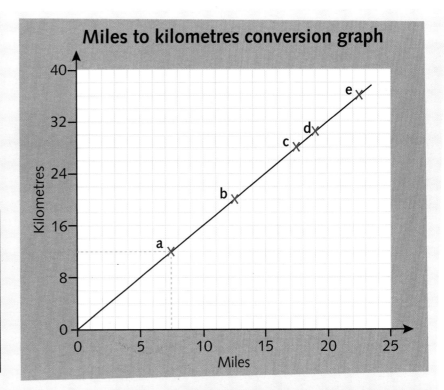

Miles to kilometres conversion graph

3 Convert these distances to kilometres.

  a 100 miles   **b** 250 miles

  c 450 miles   **d** 505 miles

> **Hint**
> If 5 miles converts to 8 kilometres, then 50 miles converts to 80 kilometres.

4 Convert these distances to miles.

  a 240 km   **b** 640 km   **c** 480 km   **d** 1,000 km

5 For each distance, write which approximate conversion is sensible and explain why.

  a 70 miles ≈ 110 km or 45 km   **b** 150 km ≈ 240 miles or 90 miles

Two couples hired a camper van for their holiday in France.

- Stewart drove the van for 50% of the total distance.
- Stewart's wife Sheila drove half as far as the combined distance driven by the other couple.
- Jack drove four times as far as his wife Jenny.
- Jenny drove the van for 64 kilometres.

  a How many kilometres did each person drive?

  b What was the total distance driven, in miles, during their holiday in France?

Multiples and factors

Identify common factors and common multiples

1 List the first six multiples of each of the numbers below. Then for each pair of numbers, circle the lowest common multiple.

a 6 9

b 12 18

c 7 4

d 10 25

e 21 14

f 30 50

g 15 20

h 5 8

2 Find all of the common multiples below 100 for each pair of numbers.

a 6, 8   b 12, 15   c 4, 13   d 2, 8

1 Write all of the factors of these sets of numbers. Find and circle the common factors of each set of numbers.

Example

16: ①, ②, ④, 8, 16
20: ①, ②, ④, 5, 10, 20

Hint
A factor is a whole number that divides exactly into another whole number.

a
24
40

b
36
64
56

c
56
80

d
35
18

e
32
48
80

f
60
102
55

g
27
42

h
27
54
108

i
35
84

2 Write the highest common factor for each set of numbers in Question 1.

3 Find a number that has at least five common factors with each of these numbers.

a 32	**b** 44	**c** 100
d 16	**e** 81	

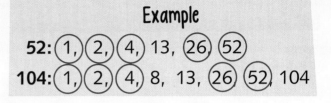

Example

52: (1,) (2,) (4,) 13, (26) (52)

104: (1,) (2,) (4,) 8, 13, (26) (52) 104

1 Find the prime factors of these numbers. Draw factor trees to help you.

a 87 **b** 232

c 185 **d** 98

e 146 **f** 356

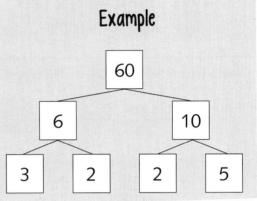

Example

```
        60
       /  \
      6    10
     / \   / \
    3   2 2   5
```

2 Describe a way of making sure you have found all of the factors of a number.

3 Copy and complete the table on the right.

- In the first column of the table write the numbers 1 to 12.

- In the second column, write any number that has that many factors.

- In the third column, write all the factors of this number.

Example

Number of factors	Number	Factors
1	1	1
2	2	1, 2
3	9	1, 3, 9
4		
5		
6		

Division ThHTO ÷ O with a remainder

- Use the formal written method of short division to calculate ThHTO ÷ O
- Estimate and check the answer to a calculation

Challenge 1

1 Find the multiple of 6 that comes immediately before each of these numbers.

 23 61 38 53 68 47 79 85

Example
16 → 12

2 Find the multiple of 8 that comes immediately before each of these numbers.

 27 68 55 92 34 39 83 95

Example
34 → 32

3 Find the multiple of 3 that comes immediately before each of these numbers.

 22 17 38 62 14 28 35 92

Example
10 → 9

4 Find the multiple of 7 that comes immediately before each of these numbers.

 79 85 23 62 54 69 85 92

Example
15 → 14

Challenge 2

Estimate the answer first, then use the formal written method to work out the answer to each calculation.
Record any answers with a remainder as a decimal and then as a fraction.

Example

$2,376 \div 5 \rightarrow 2,500 \div 5 = 500$

$$5 \overline{)2\ ^2 3\ ^3 7\ ^2 6 \cdot\ ^1 0} \quad \begin{array}{c} 4\ 7\ 5\cdot 2 \end{array} \quad \text{or } 475\tfrac{1}{5}$$

a

3,598 ÷ 5

b

5,277 ÷ 6

c
7,645 ÷ 4

d

8,664 ÷ 8

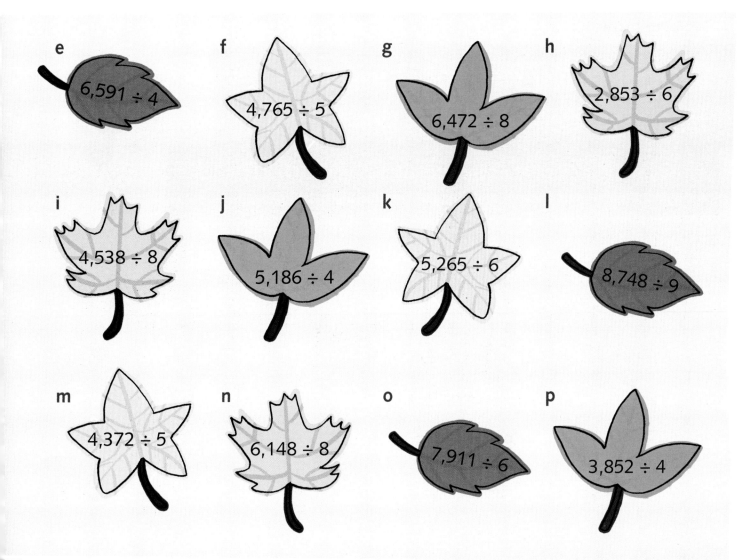

e 6,591 ÷ 4

f 4,765 ÷ 5

g 6,472 ÷ 8

h 2,853 ÷ 6

i 4,538 ÷ 8

j 5,186 ÷ 4

k 5,265 ÷ 6

l 8,748 ÷ 9

m 4,372 ÷ 5

n 6,148 ÷ 8

o 7,911 ÷ 6

p 3,852 ÷ 4

Write a calculation to match each instruction.

a Divide a 4-digit number by 6, to give an answer that includes a fraction remainder of $\frac{1}{2}$.

b Divide a 3-digit number by 9, to give an answer that includes a fraction remainder of $\frac{1}{3}$.

c Divide a 4-digit number by 5, to give an answer that ends in ·4.

d Divide a 4-digit number between 6,000 and 7,000 by 8, to give an answer that ends in ·75.

e Divide a 4-digit even number by 3 to give an answer that includes a fraction remainder of $\frac{2}{3}$.

79

Dividing ThHTO by 11 and 12 using the formal written method of short division

- Use the most efficient method to calculate ThHTO ÷ TO
- Estimate and check the answer to a calculation

Challenge 1

1 Multiply each number by 11.

Example
7 × 11 = 77

a 9 b 11 c 200 d 60 e 8

f 12 g 40 h 500 i 30 j 700

2 Multiply each number by 12.

Example
5 × 12 = 60

a 7 b 20 c 400 d 6 e 8

f 120 g 100 h 50 i 300 j 9

3 Work these calculations out mentally.

a 720 ÷ 12   b 770 ÷ 11   c 990 ÷ 11   d 360 ÷ 12

e 3,300 ÷ 11   f 6,000 ÷ 12   g 4,400 ÷ 11   h 9,600 ÷ 12

1 Sort the calculations into two groups: those you would work out mentally and those where you would use a written method.

Then work out the answer to each calculation. For those calculations that need a written method, estimate the answer first, then use the formal written method of short division.

> **Example**
> $7{,}692 \div 12$
> $\rightarrow 7{,}200 \div 12 = 600$
>
> $$\begin{array}{r} 6\ \ 4\ \ 1 \\ \hline 12\overline{)7\ {}^{7}6\ {}^{4}9\ {}^{1}2} \end{array}$$

a $432 \div 12$

b $5{,}160 \div 12$

c $5{,}566 \div 11$

d $3{,}768 \div 12$

e $4{,}741 \div 11$

f $7{,}183 \div 11$

g $2{,}880 \div 12$

h $3{,}564 \div 11$

i $3{,}696 \div 12$

j $4{,}872 \div 12$

k $396 \div 11$

l $8{,}899 \div 11$

2 Check the answer to each written calculation using the inverse method of multiplication.

1 Work out the answers to these problems.

a Eleven friends pay £2,354 between them for their ski holiday. If each person pays the same amount, how much does each person pay?

b The Jones family travel by car to their relatives. It takes them approximately 12 hours to complete the journey of 1,380 km. On average, how many kilometres per hour did they travel?

c James and William travel to Europe by car on business. They are away for 12 days and during this time travel a total of 3,246 kilometres. On average, how far did they travel each day?

d Sasha pays £6,743 for an 11-day holiday. Jamal pays £6,996 for a 12-day holiday. Who pays more per day for their holiday? How much more?

2 The answer is £503.25. What could the question be?

Solving word problems (2)

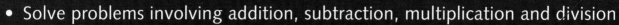

- Solve problems involving addition, subtraction, multiplication and division
- Estimate and check the answer to a calculation

Challenge 1

Look at the calculations either side of each box. Copy the calculations and use the symbol <, = or > to make each statement true.

a 631 ÷ 9   483 ÷ 4   **b** 148 ÷ 4   16 × 6

c 26 – 19   28 ÷ 4   **d** 642 ÷ 2   42 × 8

e 56 × 9   2,624 ÷ 4   **f** 540 ÷ 6   20 × 7

g 69 + 18   648 ÷ 8   **h** 63 × 7   624 – 187

i 3,535 ÷ 5   1,000 – 293   **j** 1,344 ÷ 6   14 × 16

Challenge 2

Work out the answers to these problems.

Buffet breakfast	£11
Omelette	£7
Beans on toast	£6
Cereal	£5
Coffee	£3
Tea	£2

a The café specialises in making omelettes for breakfast. They have a total of 62 dozen eggs. If each omelette uses 3 eggs, how many omelettes can be made?

b At the end of the morning, the chef calculated that he had used 696 eggs for omelettes. How many dozen eggs is this? If he started with 62 dozen, how many eggs were not used?

c 756 cups of tea and 879 cups of coffee were sold in one week. How much money was taken?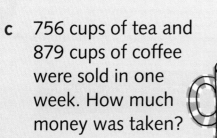

d The total earnings from buffet breakfasts for one week was £9,086. How many buffet breakfasts were sold?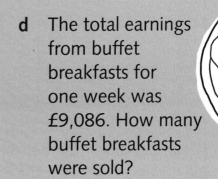

e In one week, 632 omelettes were sold and £4,656 was taken for beans on toast. Which item was most popular?

f The café has a special offer: 'Buy 2 buffet breakfasts and receive your next one half price.' Joel uses this deal to buy breakfast every day for 3 weeks. What is his total spend?

g The earnings for buffet breakfasts in one week were £5,588. The following week, the earnings increased to £8,404. How many more breakfasts were sold in the second week?

h Martin buys breakfast every day of the week. He has a buffet breakfast at the weekend, beans on toast on a Monday, an omelette on Wednesday and Friday, and cereal on each of the other days. He buys a cup of tea each weekday and a coffee both days at the weekend. How much does he spend on breakfasts in a week?

Use the information on the menu board to write your own word problems. Write the calculation you would use and the answer on another piece of paper. Give your word problems to your partner to solve. Check that your partner's answers match yours.

Seafood salad	£12
Chicken salad sandwich	£11
Salad with garlic bread	£9
Soup	£6
French fries	£4
Cold drinks	£2.50
Hot drinks	£3

Fraction and decimal equivalents (1)

Associate a fraction with division and calculate decimal fraction equivalents

Challenge 1

1 Copy each number line, then complete it choosing decimals from the number cards below. Some decimals will be used more than once.

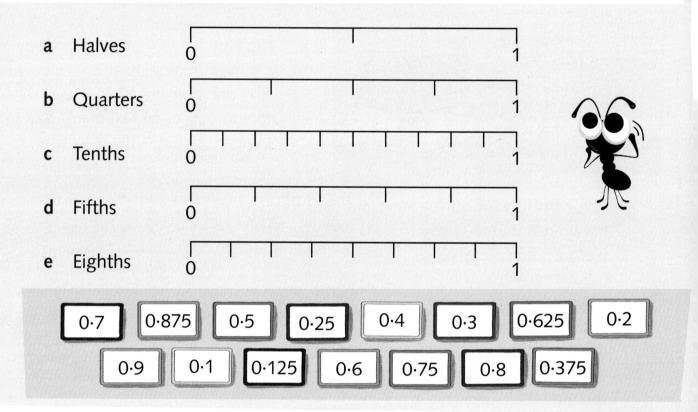

a Halves 0 ——— 1

b Quarters 0 ——— 1

c Tenths 0 ——— 1

d Fifths 0 ——— 1

e Eighths 0 ——— 1

| 0·7 | 0·875 | 0·5 | 0·25 | 0·4 | 0·3 | 0·625 | 0·2 |

| 0·9 | 0·1 | 0·125 | 0·6 | 0·75 | 0·8 | 0·375 |

2 Complete the fraction wall on Resource 22: Fraction wall (1). What fractions are equivalent to the decimal fractions you have written? Try to remember all the equivalences and write them down.

You will need:
• Resource 22: Fraction wall (1)

3 Copy and complete these calculations.

a 0·5 + ☐ = 1

b 0·25 + ☐ + ☐ + ☐ = 1

c 0·1 + 0·1 + ☐ + ☐ + ☐ + ☐ + ☐ + ☐ + ☐ + ☐ = 1

d 0·2 + ☐ + ☐ + ☐ + ☐ = 1

e 0·125 + 0·125 + ☐ + ☐ + ☐ + ☐ + ☐ + ☐ = 1

1 Using Resource 3: Number lines, write in the appropriate fractions or decimals. On some lines, not all the scale marks will need a value.

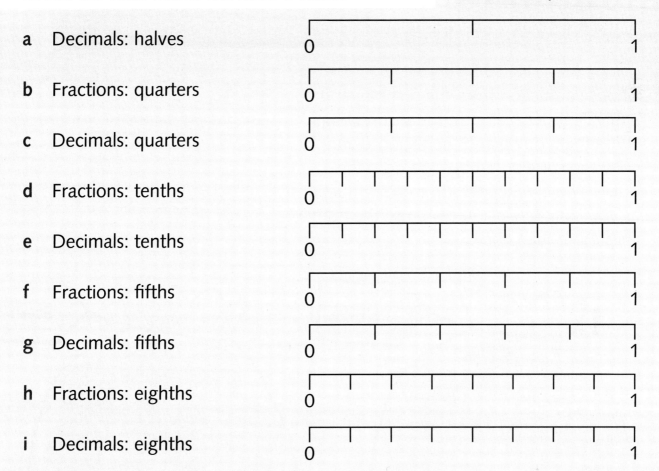

a   Decimals: halves

b   Fractions: quarters

c   Decimals: quarters

d   Fractions: tenths

e   Decimals: tenths

f   Fractions: fifths

g   Decimals: fifths

h   Fractions: eighths

i   Decimals: eighths

2 Look at all your number lines from Question 1. Using coloured pencils, circle the fractions and decimals that are equivalent.
Can you find any groups of three that are equivalent?

1 Explain clearly why $\frac{1}{8} = 0.125$. Read your explanation to a partner. Ask them to give you some feedback about how well you have explained the maths.

2 What decimal is equivalent to each of the fractions below? Explain to a partner how you worked them out.

$\frac{1}{20}$ $\frac{5}{20}$ $\frac{13}{20}$ $\frac{15}{20}$ $\frac{19}{20}$

3 What do you notice about the decimal equivalents for these two fractions? Why is this?

$\frac{1}{3}$ $\frac{2}{3}$

Fraction and decimal equivalents (2)

Associate a fraction with division and calculate decimal fraction equivalents

Choose a fraction from the first bag and an equivalent decimal from the second bag. Write them down and then choose and copy the correct number line from the options below. Repeat for as many fractions as you can. You will need to use the number lines more than once.

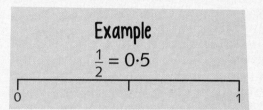

Example

$$\frac{1}{2} = 0.5$$

0 ⸻ 1

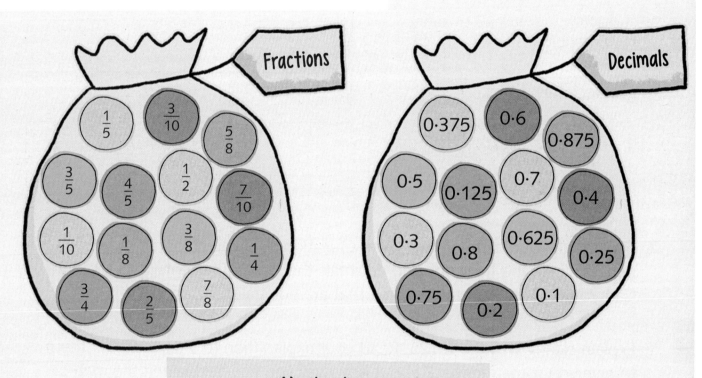

Fractions

$\frac{1}{5}$ $\frac{3}{10}$ $\frac{5}{8}$ $\frac{3}{5}$ $\frac{4}{5}$ $\frac{1}{2}$ $\frac{7}{10}$ $\frac{1}{10}$ $\frac{1}{8}$ $\frac{3}{8}$ $\frac{1}{4}$ $\frac{3}{4}$ $\frac{2}{5}$ $\frac{7}{8}$

Decimals

0.375 0.6 0.875 0.5 0.125 0.7 0.4 0.3 0.625 0.8 0.25 0.75 0.2 0.1

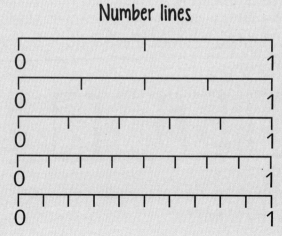

Number lines

0 ⸻ 1

0 ⸻ 1

0 ⸻ 1

0 ⸻ 1

0 ⸻ 1

1 For each fraction, write a calculation to find its decimal equivalent and then work it out. Check your answers using a calculator.

You will need:
• calculator

a $\frac{1}{2}$ b $\frac{1}{4}$ c $\frac{3}{4}$ d $\frac{1}{5}$ e $\frac{3}{10}$

f $\frac{7}{10}$ g $\frac{2}{5}$ h $\frac{3}{8}$ i $\frac{4}{5}$ j $\frac{4}{10}$

> **Example**
> $\frac{1}{2} = 1 \div 2 = 0.5$

2 Write these fractions in two groups under the headings 'Less than half' and 'More than half'.

$\frac{3}{9}$ $\frac{7}{12}$ $\frac{2}{7}$ $\frac{1}{3}$ $\frac{4}{7}$ $\frac{2}{11}$ $\frac{5}{12}$ $\frac{8}{9}$ $\frac{6}{15}$ $\frac{8}{13}$ $\frac{2}{3}$ $\frac{6}{7}$

3 Change each fraction in Question 2 to a decimal to check if you were correct.

4 Explain why the numerator divided by the denominator in a fraction is the way to find the decimal equivalent.

I can check that $\frac{7}{9}$ is more than half as the decimal equivalent is 0·777,777,78 and this is greater than 0·5.

---

1 Work out the decimal equivalent for each fraction. What do you notice about the decimals? Why do ninths make this pattern?

$\frac{1}{9}$ $\frac{2}{9}$ $\frac{3}{9}$ $\frac{4}{9}$ $\frac{5}{9}$ $\frac{6}{9}$ $\frac{7}{9}$ $\frac{8}{9}$

You will need:
• calculator

2 Work out the decimal equivalent for each fraction. Round each one to a decimal number with 3 places.

> **Example**
> $\frac{2}{7} = 2 \div 7 = 0.285,714,3$
> $\frac{2}{7} = 0.286$

a $\frac{4}{7}$ b $\frac{6}{13}$ c $\frac{3}{14}$ d $\frac{7}{12}$

e $\frac{9}{11}$ f $\frac{1}{17}$ g $\frac{2}{3}$ h $\frac{6}{7}$

As the 7 in my decimal equivalent is larger than 5, I have to round the thousandths digit up to 6. So $\frac{2}{7}$ to 3 decimal places is 0·286.

Fractions, decimals and percentages (1)

Recall and use equivalences between fractions, decimals and percentages

Challenge 1

1 Write the fraction and the decimal that are equivalent to each percentage.

Example

$$13\% = \frac{13}{100} = 0\cdot13$$

Remember they are all hundredths.

a 1%   b 25%   c 7%   d 24%   e 36%

f 41%   g 55%   h 63%   i 79%   j 86%

k 92%   l 99%   m 11%   n 19%   o 48%

p 57%   q 68%   r 5%   s 37%   t 71%

2 What is the relationship between fractions, decimals and percentages?

Challenge 2

1 Work out the decimal equivalent and two fraction equivalents for each percentage.

a 25%   b 80%   c 50%   d 30%   e 75%

f 40%   g 20%   h 60%   i 10%   j 90%

2 Write the percentage, fraction and decimal equivalents that are hidden in the clouds.

Example

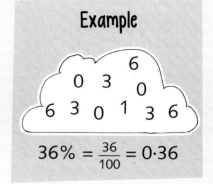

$36\% = \frac{36}{100} = 0.36$

a

b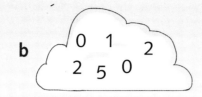

c
```
    3
  0 8  0
3 8 0 1 8 3
```

d
```
  7 5 0
  5 3 7 4
```

e
```
        9
    0 2 0
  9 2 0 1 2 9
```

f
```
      1
  0 1
  0 1 1 0
```

g
```
      2
  4   1 0
  5 2   5
```

h
```
  0   6 5
    6   1 0
  5 0   6 5
```

i
```
    6
  0   3
  5 0   6
```

j
```
      1
  0 1   0
1 3 0 1 3 3
```

k
```
      2
  0 2 0
2 2 0 1 2 2
```

1 Work out the decimal and simplified fraction equivalent for each percentage.

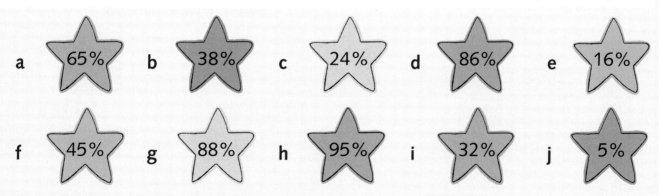

a 65% **b** 38% **c** 24% **d** 86% **e** 16%

f 45% **g** 88% **h** 95% **i** 32% **j** 5%

2 Many people refer to one third as 33% and two thirds as 66%.
Is this mathematically correct? Explain your answer.

Calculating percentages

Solve problems involving the calculation of percentages and the use of percentages for comparison

Challenge 1

1 Work out these percentages.

a 50% of 1,600 b 50% of 3,000 c 25% of 4,000

d 10% of 3,800 e 10% of 5,100 f 30% of 6,200

g 40% of 5,300 h 70% of 7,100 i 50% of 1,400

2 Use the information in the yellow box to answer the questions.

• 1,200 people went to a show.
• Ticket sales raised: £3,400.
• Programme sales raised: £2,800.

a 25% of the total money raised was given to charity. How much money was given to charity?

b 40% of the audience were children. How many children were there?

c 12% of people arrived by bus, 27% arrived by car, 36% walked and the rest came by train. What percentage of people came by train? How many people came by train?

Challenge 2

1 For each question, work out the percentages of the number in the middle.

Remember, one way to work out the answer is to find 1% and multiply the result by the per cent you want to find.

a 30% 25%
   7,800
   18% 80%

b 23% 75%
   8,100
   49% 60%

c 61% 40%
   9,300
   5% 79%

d 46% 20%
   8,800
   65% 11%

e 90% 36%
   9,700
   53% 3%

f 13% 20%
   12,500
   75% 99%

2 What is an efficient way to work out 99%?

3 Use the information in the yellow box to answer the questions.

> - 6,400 people went to a concert.
> - Ticket sales raised: £9,800.
> - Ice-cream sales raised: £2,800.

   a 45% of the ticket sales was used to pay the band. How much money was that?

   b Of the people who bought ice creams, 35% bought strawberry, 44% bought chocolate and the rest bought vanilla. How much money was raised from the sale of vanilla ice creams?

   c 800 programmes were sold throughout the evening. Halfway through the evening, 70% of the programmes had been sold at 80p each. The price of the remaining programmes was reduced by 10% and they were all sold. What was the total amount of money raised by selling programmes?

   d At the end of the concert, 5% of people drove home, 25% caught a bus, 42% walked and the rest caught a train. How many travelled by each mode of transport?

enge
3

1 For each question, work out the percentages of the number in the middle. Some of your answers will be decimals.

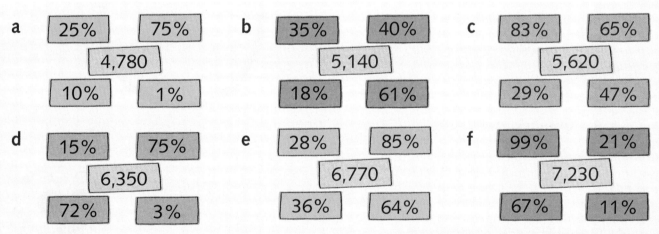

a 25% 75% 4,780 10% 1%

b 35% 40% 5,140 18% 61%

c 83% 65% 5,620 29% 47%

d 15% 75% 6,350 72% 3%

e 28% 85% 6,770 36% 64%

f 99% 21% 7,230 67% 11%

2 The information in the yellow box describes how the money raised for a charity concert was spent. Use the information to answer the questions.

> - 5% was spent on printing the programmes.
> - 36% was used to pay the band.
> - 10% was used to pay the staff.
> - 24% was given to charity.
> - There was £2,450 left, which was 25% of the money raised.

   a How much money was raised altogether?

   b How was the money divided between each of the three expenses and the charity?

Converting units of time

Convert from smaller to larger units of time and vice versa

Challenge 1

1 Convert each of these times to minutes.

    a 1 h 40 min   **b** 2 h 20 min   **c** 4 h 30 min   **d** 3 h 16 min

2 Convert each of these times to hours and minutes.

    a 90 min   **b** 160 min   **c** 200 min   **d** 165 min

3 Convert these times to the units given.

    a 95 s to minutes and seconds

    b 2 min 40 s to seconds

    c 3 days to hours

    d 50 h to days and hours

    e 4 weeks to days

    f 40 days to weeks and days

    g 6 years to months

    h 50 months to years and months

Challenge 2

1 Convert each of these times to minutes.

    a 3 h 25 min   **b** 5 h 42 min   **c** 10 h 37 min

    d 12 h 14 min   **e** 1 day   **f** 1 week

2 Convert each of these times to hours and minutes.

    a 250 min   **b** 400 min   **c** 505 min   **d** 1,000 min

3 Convert these times to the units given.

   a 144 s to minutes and seconds   **b** 9 min 48 s to seconds

   c 7 days to hours   **d** 75 h to days and hours

   e 13 weeks to days   **f** 130 days to weeks and days

   g 8 years to months   **h** 80 months to years and months

   i 10 years to weeks   **j** 100 weeks to years and weeks

4 How many:

   a seconds in 1 hour?

   b minutes in 1 day?

   c hours in 1 week?

5 If your heart beats once every second, how many times will it beat in a day?

1 Copy and complete the table.

Hours (h)	0·1	0·2	0·3	0·4	0·5
Minutes (min)	6				

2 Convert each of these times to hours and minutes.

   a 3·4 h   **b** 2·7 h   **c** 5·8 h   **d** 3·6 h

3 Convert these times to hours using decimals.

   a 2 h 18 min   **b** 7 h 42 min   **c** 9 h 54 min   **d** 12 h 12 min

4 How long is:

   a 1 million seconds in completed days?

   b 1 million minutes in completed weeks?

   c 1 million hours in completed years?

Problems involving time

Calculate and convert between units of time to solve problems

Challenge 1

Use the table to answer these questions.

Swimming pool opening hours		
Day	**Opening time**	**Closing time**
Sun	10:00 a.m.	5:00 p.m.
Mon–Fri	7:30 a.m.	9:00 p.m.
Sat	9:00 a.m.	6:00 p.m.

1 On which day or days is the pool open for nine hours?

2 For how many hours is the pool open on a Wednesday?

3 On Sunday, Garry arrived at the leisure centre at 9:47 a.m. How many minutes did he have to wait until the swimming pool opened?

4 On Friday, Helen left the swimming pool at 20:23. How many minutes after she left did the pool close?

5 Iain swims for 45 minutes every day except Sunday. How much time, in hours and minutes, does he spend in the pool each week?

Challenge 2

1 The leisure centre is holding a swimming event to raise money for charity.

a Year 6 enters a team of eight swimmers in the relay event. Each swimmer, in turn, completes 4 lengths of the pool in an average time of 50 seconds per length. How many minutes and seconds does the team take to complete their swim?

b Melissa completed 4 lengths of the pool in 3 minutes and 40 seconds. If she continued to swim at this rate, how long would it take her to complete 20 lengths of the pool?

c Nico swam 24 lengths of the pool in 19 minutes. If he completed his swim at 11:07 a.m., at what time did he begin his first length of the pool?

2 There are exactly 6 weeks to the end of the school term.
After 10 days, how many days will there be until the end of term?

3 On your 12th birthday, how many weeks old are you?

4 At Bert's Bakery, Bert makes apple pies and custard pies.

- The apple pies are baked for 25 minutes and the custard pies are baked for 20 minutes.

- As each tray of pies is finished, it is taken from the oven and a new tray is put in.

- At 11:15 a.m. Bert puts one tray of apple pies and one tray of custard pies into the oven.

When is the next time that Bert puts a tray of apple pies and a tray of custard pies into the oven at the same time?

5 One day on planet Earth lasts 24 hours.
Tom spends one quarter of each day at school.
Calculate the number of hours and minutes
Tom would spend at school each day if he lived
on each of these planets and spent one quarter
of his day at school.

Planet	Mercury	Venus	Earth	Mars	Jupiter	Uranus	Pluto*
Hours in 1 day	59	243	24	25	10	17	153

*Pluto is a dwarf planet

nge

Using the table in Question 5 of Challenge 2,
calculate the number of hours and minutes
you would spend asleep on each of the
planets each day if you slept for the same
fraction of time as you do on Earth.

Finding the average speed

Calculate speed using compound units

Challenges
1, 2

1 Work out each speed.

  a 40 km in 1 hour   **b** 25 miles in 1 hour

  c 5 km in 1 hour   **d** 62 km in 1 hour

  e 500 miles in 1 hour   **f** 14 km in 1 hour

> **Example**
>
> 30 km in 1 hour = 30 km/h
> 20 miles in 1 hour = 20 mph

2 Calculate the average speed of each motorcyclist in kilometres per hour.

> **Example**
>
> 90 km in 3 hours
> Speed = 90 ÷ 3
>   = 30 km/h

a

100 km in 2 hours

b

160 km in 4 hours

c

240 km in 6 hours

d

150 km in 5 hours

e

105 km in 3 hours

Challenge
2

1 Calculate the average speed of each lorry in miles per hour.

a

120 miles in 4 hours

b

225 miles in 5 hours

c

210 miles in 6 hours

2 Calculate the average speed of each vehicle in kilometres per hour.

a

20 km in $\frac{1}{4}$ hour

b

15 km in $\frac{1}{2}$ hour

Example

12 km in $\frac{1}{2}$ hour

24 km in 1 hour

Speed = 24 km/h

c

7·5 km in $\frac{1}{2}$ hour

d

2·5 km in $\frac{1}{3}$ hour

e

1·2 km in $\frac{1}{5}$ hour

3 Double each distance in Question 2 and write the new speed.

4 The speed limit for a lorry is 60 mph. If the driver travels 220 miles in 4 hours, how does the actual average speed compare to its speed limit?

1 A long-distance lorry driver travels on the motorway at an average speed of 80 kilometres per hour. Copy and complete the table.

Time (h)	$\frac{1}{4}$	$\frac{1}{2}$	1	2	3	4
Distance (km)			80			

2 A container ship crosses the North Sea at an average speed of 18 kilometres per hour. Copy and complete the table.

Time (h)			1			
Distance (km)	4·5	9	18	36	54	72

Calculating speed

Calculate speed using compound units

Challenge 1

1 Write each speed using the correct unit of speed in each answer.

Example
50 cm in 1 minute
Speed = 50 cm/min

   a 17 m in 1 second   **b** 30 cm in 1 minute

   c 900 m in 1 hour   **d** 7 cm in 1 second

2 Calculate the average speed of each of the following:

Example
45 cm in 5 minutes
Speed = 9 cm/min

   a swallow: 3,500 m in 7 minutes

   b tortoise: 300 cm in 15 minutes

   c sheep: 360 m in 30 minutes

   d snail: 3·9 cm in 3 seconds

   e grizzly bear: 330 m in 5 minutes

   f cheetah: 3·2 km in 2 minutes

Challenge 2

1 Three children were timed swimming.

- Matt swam 500 m in 4 minutes.

- Leon swam 450 m in 5 minutes.

- Ken swam 600 m in 6 minutes.

   a Calculate the average speed of each swimmer in metres per minute.

   b List the swimmers in order, from fastest to slowest.

2 Calculate each average speed in metres per hour and then in kilometres per hour.

Example
420 m in 15 minutes
(420 m × 4) in 1 hour
Speed = 1,680 m/h
= 1·68 km/h

   a 800 m in 30 minutes   **b** 500 m in 15 minutes

   c 250 m in 10 minutes   **d** 350 m in 20 minutes

   e 1,300 m in 15 minutes   **f** 740 m in 6 minutes

3 Three aeroplanes flew the following distances:

- Aeroplane A flew 2,268 miles in 4 hours.

- Aeroplane B flew 2,735 miles in 5 hours.

- Aeroplane C flew 3,180 miles in 6 hours.

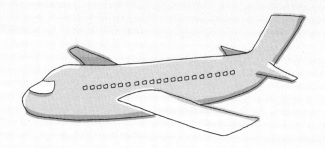

a Calculate the average speed of each aircraft in miles per hour.

b If Aeroplane A flew for 6 hours at the same average speed, how many more miles would it have travelled than Aeroplane C?

4 A glacier in the French Alps moved 168 cm in one week. What was its average speed in centimetres per day?

5 In 2012, the Jakobshavn Glacier in Greenland was recorded as moving at about 40 metres per day. If the glacier had continued to move at this speed, what would its speed have been in kilometres per year?

1 Light travels at approximately 186,000 miles per second.

a How many miles will light travel in 5 seconds?

b The Earth is 93 million miles from the sun. Find how long it takes the light from the sun to travel to Earth in:

i seconds
ii minutes to one decimal place

2 Mercury is 57 million miles from the sun. How many minutes, to the nearest minute, will it take the light from the sun to reach Mercury?

Maths facts

Addition and subtraction

Whole numbers

Example: 456,287 + 359,849

```
    4 5 6 2 8 7
 +  3 5 9 8 4 9
    8 1 6 1 3 6
    1 1 1 1
```

Example: 746,291 − 298,354

```
  6 13 15 12  8 11
  7 ̶4 ̶6 ̶2 ̶9 ̶1
 − 2 9 8 3 5 4
   4 4 7 9 3 7
```

```
  6 13 15  1  8  1
  7 ̶4 ̶6 ̶2 ̶9  1
 − 2 9 8 3 5 4
   4 4 7 9 3 7
```

> You can also write the exchanged values like this.

Decimals

Example: 57·486 + 45·378

```
    5 7 · 4 8 6
 +  4 5 · 3 7 8
  1 0 2 · 8 6 4
    1       1 1
```

Example: 63·237 − 45·869

```
  5 12  11 12 17
  6 ̶3 · ̶2 ̶3 ̶7
 − 4 5 · 8 6 9
   1 7 · 3 6 8
```

```
  5 12  11 12  1
  6 ̶3 · ̶2 ̶3  7
 − 4 5 · 8 6 9
   1 7 · 3 6 8
```

> You can also write the exchanged values like this.

Multiplication and division

Written methods – short multiplication

Whole numbers

Example: 2,654 × 3

Partitioning

$2{,}654 \times 3 = (2{,}000 \times 3) + (600 \times 3) + (50 \times 3) + (4 \times 3)$
$= 6{,}000 + 1{,}800 + 150 + 12$
$= 7{,}962$

Grid method

×	2,000	600	50	4	
3	6,000	1,800	150	12	= 7,962

Expanded written method

```
    2 6 5 4
 ×        3
        1 2   (4 × 3)
      1 5 0   (50 × 3)
    1 8 0 0   (600 × 3)
    6 0 0 0   (2,000 × 3)
    7 9 6 2
```

Formal written method

```
    2 6 5 4
 ×        3
    7 9 6 2
    1 1 1
```

```
        2 6 5 4
 ×  1 1 1     3
    7 9 6 2
```

> You can also write the regrouped values like this.

Decimals

Example: 4·83 × 6

Partitioning

$4{\cdot}83 \times 6 = (4 \times 6) + (0{\cdot}8 \times 6) + (0{\cdot}03 \times 6)$
$= 24 + 4{\cdot}8 + 0{\cdot}18$
$= 28{\cdot}98$

Grid method

×	4	0.8	0.03	
6	24	4.8	0.18	= 28.98

Expanded written method

```
      4 · 8 3
 ×          6
      0 · 1 8   (0·03 × 6)
      4 · 8 0   (0·8 × 6)
    2 4 · 0 0   (4 × 6)
    2 8 · 9 8
```

Formal written method

```
      4 · 8 3
 ×          6
    2 8 · 9 8
      4   1
```

We can also work out the answer to this calculation by converting the decimal to a whole number before calculating, then converting the product back to a decimal 4·83 × 6 is equivalent to 483 × 6 ÷ 100

Written methods – long multiplication
Whole numbers

Example: 285 × 63

Partitioning

285 × 63 = (200 × 63) + (80 × 63) + (5 × 63)
$\qquad$ = 12,600 + 5,040 + 315
$\qquad$ = 17,955

Grid method

×	200	80	5
60	12,000	4,800	300
3	600	240	15

$\qquad$ 17100
+ $\quad$ 855
$\overline{\qquad 17955}$

Expanded written method

```
      2 8 5
  ×     6 3
  ─────────
      1 5    (5 × 3)
      2 4 0  (80 × 3)
      6 0 0  (200 × 3)
      3 0 0  (5 × 60)
    4 8 0 0  (80 × 60)
  1 2 0 0 0  (200 × 60)
  ─────────
  1 7 9 5 5
      1
```

Formal written method

```
      2 8 5
  ×     6 3
  ─────────
    8² 5¹ 5   (285 × 3)
  1 7⁵ 1³ 0 0 (285 × 60)
  ─────────
  1 7 9 5 5
```

Decimals

Example: 7·56 × 34

Partitioning

7·56 × 34 = (7 × 34) + (0·5 × 34) + (0·06 × 34)
$\qquad$ = 238 + 17 + 2·04
$\qquad$ = 257·04

Grid method

×	7	0·5	0·06
30	210	15	1·8
4	28	2	0·24

$\qquad$ 226·80
+ $\quad$ 30·24
$\overline{\qquad 257·04}$

Expanded written method

```
      7 · 5 6
  ×       3 4
  ───────────
      0 · 2 4  (0·06 × 4)
      2 · 0 0  (0·5 × 4)
    2 8 · 0 0  (7 × 4)
      1 · 8 0  (0·06 × 30)
    1 5 · 0 0  (0·5 × 30)
  2 1 0 · 0 0  (7 × 30)
  ───────────
  2 5 7 · 0 4
      1   1
```

Formal written method

```
      7 · 5 6
  ×       3 4
  ───────────
    3 0² · 2² 4  (7·56 × 4)
  2 2¹ 6¹ · 8 0  (7·56 × 30)
  ───────────
  2 5 7 · 0 4
        1
```

We can also work out the answer to this calculation by converting the decimal to a whole number before calculating, then converting the product back to a decimal.

7·56 × 34 is equivalent to 756 × 34 ÷ 100

101

Written methods – short division
Whole numbers
Example: 1,838 ÷ 8

Expanded written method

```
        2 2 9  r 6
    8)1 8 3 8
    - 1 6 0 0    (200 × 8)
      ¹2 ¹3 8
    -   1 6 0    (20 × 8)
          7 8
    -     7 2    (9 × 8)
            6
```

Formal written method

Whole number remainder	Fraction remainder
$\;\;2\;2\;9\,\text{r}\,6$ $8\overline{)1\,^18\,^23\,^78}$	$\;\;2\;2\;9\frac{3}{4}$ $8\overline{)1\,^18\,^23\,^78}$

Decimal remainder

```
        2 2 9 · 7 5
    8)1 ¹8 ²3 ⁷8 ·⁶0 ⁴0
```

Decimals
Example: 45·36 ÷ 6

Regrouping

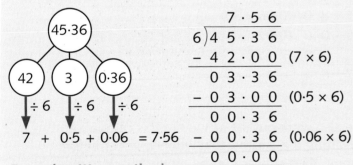

7 + 0·5 + 0·06 = 7·56

Expanded written method

```
        7 · 5 6
    6)4 5 · 3 6
    - 4 2 · 0 0    (7 × 6)
      0 3 · 3 6
    - 0 3 · 0 0    (0·5 × 6)
      0 0 · 3 6
    - 0 0 · 3 6    (0·06 × 6)
      0 0 · 0 0
```

Formal written method

```
        7 · 5 6
    6)4 ⁴5 ·³3 ³6
```

We can also work out the answer to this calculation by converting the decimal to a whole number before calculating, then converting the product back to a decimal.

45·36 ÷ 6 is equivalent to 4,536 ÷ 6 ÷ 100

Written methods – long division
Whole numbers
Example: 8,548 ÷ 16

Expanded written method	Formal written method

`    5 3 4  r 4`
 `16)8 5 4 8`
 `- 8 0 0 0   (500 × 16)`
 `  ⁴5 ¹4 8`
 `-   4 8 0   (30 × 16)`
 `      6 8`
 `-     6 4   (4 × 16)`
 `        4`
	`    5 3 4  r 4`
	 `16)8 5 4 8`
	 `- 8 0 ↓`
	 `  ⁴5 ¹4`
	 `-   4 8 ↓`
	 `      6 8`
	 `-     6 4`
	 `        4`

8,468 ÷ 16 = 534 r 4 or $534\frac{1}{4}$ or 534·25

Decimals
Example: 45·64 ÷ 14

Expanded written method

```
         3 · 2 6
    14)4 5 · 6 4
    -  4 2 · 0 0    (3 × 14)
       0 ²3 ·¹6 4
    -  0 2 · 8 0    (0·2 × 14)
       0 0 · 8 4
    -  0 0 · 8 4    (0·06 × 14)
       0 0 · 0 0
```

Formal written method

```
         3 · 2 6
    14)4 5 · 6 4
    -  4 2 · ↓
       ²3 ·¹6
    -    2 · 8 ↓
         0 · 8 4
    -    0 · 8 4
         0 · 0 0
```

We can also work out the answer to this calculation by converting the decimal to a whole number before calculating, then converting the product back to a decimal.

45·64 ÷ 14 is equivalent to 4,564 ÷ 14 ÷ 100

Fractions, decimals and percentages

$$\frac{1}{100} = 0\cdot01 = 1\%$$ $$\frac{2}{100} = \frac{1}{50} = 0\cdot02 = 2\%$$ $$\frac{4}{100} = \frac{1}{25} = 0\cdot04 = 4\%$$

$$\frac{5}{100} = \frac{1}{20} = 0\cdot05 = 5\%$$ $$\frac{10}{100} = \frac{1}{10} = 0\cdot1 = 10\%$$ $$\frac{20}{100} = \frac{1}{5} = 0\cdot2 = 20\%$$

$$\frac{25}{100} = \frac{1}{4} = 0\cdot25 = 25\%$$ $$\frac{40}{100} = \frac{2}{5} = 0\cdot4 = 40\%$$ $$\frac{50}{100} = \frac{1}{2} = 0\cdot5 = 50\%$$

$$\frac{75}{100} = \frac{3}{4} = 0\cdot75 = 75\%$$ $$\frac{80}{100} = \frac{4}{5} = 0\cdot8 = 80\%$$ $$\frac{100}{100} = \frac{10}{10} = 1 = 100\%$$

Add proper fractions   Subtract proper fractions

$$\frac{1}{3} + \frac{2}{5} = \frac{5}{15} + \frac{6}{15}$$ $$\frac{9}{10} - \frac{2}{3} = \frac{27}{30} - \frac{20}{30}$$ $$\frac{2}{3} \times 4 = \frac{8}{3}$$ $$2\frac{3}{4} \times 3 = \frac{11}{4} \times 3$$

$$= \frac{11}{15}$$ $$= \frac{7}{30}$$ $$= 2\frac{2}{3}$$ $$= \frac{33}{4}$$

$$= 8\frac{1}{4}$$

Add mixed numbers

$$1\frac{2}{3} + 2\frac{3}{4} = 3 + \frac{2}{3} + \frac{3}{4}$$ or $$1\frac{2}{3} + 2\frac{3}{4} = \frac{5}{3} + \frac{11}{4}$$

$$= 3 + \frac{8}{12} + \frac{9}{12}$$ $$= \frac{20}{12} + \frac{33}{12}$$

$$= 3\frac{17}{12}$$ $$= \frac{53}{12}$$

$$= 4\frac{5}{12}$$ $$= 4\frac{5}{12}$$

Subtract mixed numbers

$$3\frac{1}{5} - 1\frac{2}{3} = 3\frac{3}{15} - 1\frac{10}{15}$$ or $$3\frac{1}{5} - 1\frac{2}{3} = \frac{16}{5} - \frac{5}{3}$$

$$= 2\frac{18}{15} - 1\frac{10}{15}$$ $$= \frac{48}{15} - \frac{25}{15}$$

$$= 1\frac{8}{15}$$ $$= \frac{23}{15}$$

$$= 1\frac{8}{15}$$

Multiply two proper fractions   Divide a proper fraction by a whole number

$$\frac{3}{4} \times \frac{1}{3} = \frac{3}{12} = \frac{1}{4}$$ $$\frac{2}{3} \div 5 = \frac{2}{3} \times \frac{1}{5} = \frac{2}{15}$$

Measurement

Length

1 km = 1,000 m = 100,000 cm
0·1 km = 100 m = 10,000 cm = 100,000 mm
0·01 km = 10 m = 1,000 cm = 10,000 mm
1 m = 100 cm = 1,000 mm
0·1 m = 10 cm = 100 mm

0·01 m = 1 cm = 10 mm
0·001 m = 0·1 cm = 1 mm
1 cm = 10 mm
0·1 cm = 1 mm

Metric units and imperial units – Length

1 km $\approx \frac{5}{8}$ miles (8 km $\approx$ 5 miles)

1 inch $\approx$ 2·5 cm

Capacity

1 litre = 1,000 ml
0·1 l = 100 ml
0·01 l = 10 ml
0·001 l = 1 ml
1 cl = 10 ml

24-hour time

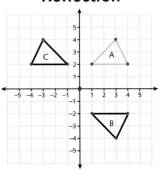

Perimeter, area and volume

P = perimeter   A = area   V = volume
l = length w = width b = base h = height

Perimeter of a rectangle

$P = 2(l + w)$

Perimeter of a square

$P = 4 \times l$ or $P = 4l$

Area of a rectangle

$A = l \times w$ or $A = lw$

Area of a triangle

$A = \frac{1}{2} \times b \times h$ or $A = \frac{1}{2}bh$

Area of a parallelogram

$A = b \times h$ or $A = bh$

Volume of a cuboid

$V = l \times w \times h$ or $V = lwh$

Mass

1 t = 1,000 kg   1 kg = 1,000 g   0·1 kg = 100 g   0·01 kg = 10 g   0·001 kg = 1 g

Geometry

Parts of a circle

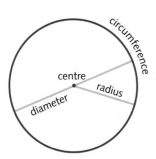

Coordinates

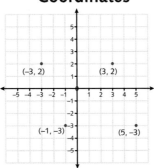

Translation

Shape A has been translated 8 squares to the right and 5 squares up.

Reflection

Shape A has been reflected in the x-axis (Shape B) and in the y-axis (Shape C).